STRESS MANAGEMENT FOR EDUCATORS

A Guide To Manage Your Response To Stress

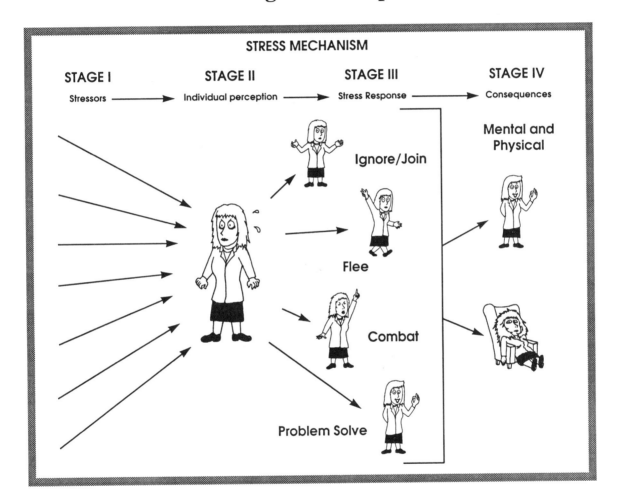

STRESS MECHANISM

STAGE I	STAGE II	STAGE III	STAGE IV
Stressors ⟶	Individual perception ⟶	Stress Response ⟶	Consequences

Ignore/Join

Flee

Combat

Problem Solve

Mental and Physical

By Bettie B. Youngs, Ph.D.

J

JALMAR PRESS
ROLLING HILLS ESTATES, CALIFORNIA

Stress Management for Educators
A Guide to Manage Your Response to Stress

Copyright © 1993 by Bettie B. Youngs, Ph.D.

> Jalmar Press
> Permissions Dept.
> Skypark Business Center
> 2675 Skypark Drive, Suite 204
> Torrance, CA 90505-5330
> (310) 784-0016   FAX: (310) 784-1379

Library of Congress Cataloging-in-Publication Data

Youngs, Bettie B.
     Stress management for educators. A guide to manage
     your response to stress. / Bettie B. Youngs
          p. cm.
     Includes bibliographical references
     ISBN 0-915190-77-X : $12.95
     1. Teachers — United States — Attitudes.   2. Self-Esteem — United States.   I. Title.
     LB1775.2.Y68   1993   90-52732
     371.1'001'9 — dc20   CIP

Published by Jalmar Press

STRESS MANAGEMENT FOR EDUCATORS
A Guide to Manage Your Response to Stress

Author: Bettie B. Youngs
Editor: Marie Conte
Production Consultants: Mario A. Artavia II and Jeanne Iler
Cover Design: Mario A. Artavia II
Typography: Mario A. Artavia II
Manufactured in the United States of America
First edition printing: 10 9 8 7 6 5 4 3 2 1

STRESS MANAGEMENT FOR EDUCATORS

A Guide to Manage Your Response to Stress

Virtually no one feels free of stress these days, certainly not educators with too much to do and too little time to do it! Hardly a day goes by when educators are not pressured and stretched to capacity. In today's educational arena, stress seems to be accepted — an "occupational hazard." But that doesn't mean you have to suffer the consequences. You *must* manage it so as not to endanger the health and productivity of yourself as well as your students and fellow colleagues.

Stress! Everyone experiences it, but how much do *you* know about it? What is stress? What causes it? How do you respond to it? What can be done to manage stress, to moderate its negative effects? Can stress be used to your advantage? How can we stress-proof educators and help them remain at peak performance?

This manual answers those questions, providing useful information and practical suggestions for you, the educator. This book is designed to help you:

- Examine the nature of stress and its impact on you, your classroom and school environment, your students, and your productivity
- Identify physical, emotional and behavioral manifestations of stress
- Identify factors in the schoolplace that commonly produce stress, and ways to minimize their negative aspects
- Identify individual factors producing stress for you and assess how you respond to them
- Learn key intervention and prevention strategies to manage stress

Each of us interprets and assigns different meanings (power) to stressful situations. How violently or calmly you respond to stress itself is under *your* control. You get to decide. Many professionally effective and personally powerful people, recognizing that the power to do so lies within themselves, are able to manage stress and turn it their advantage. The question then is not whether to eliminate stress altogether (a difficult if not impossible goal) but how to manage it — or rather, manage our *response* to it. The goal is to use stress constructively to promote health, self-development, and productivity.

Bettie B. Youngs

Bettie B. Youngs, Ph.D.

About the Author

Bettie B. Youngs, Ph.D. is an internationally known lecturer, author, counselor and consultant. Her work has spanned more than sixty countries for more than two decades, earning her a reputation as a respected authority in the field of personal and professional effectiveness. She has earned national acclaim for her work on the effects of stress on health, wellness, and productivity for both adults and children, and for her work on the role of self-esteem as it detracts from or empowers vitality, achievement, and peak performance. Dr. Youngs has conducted extensive research on the stages of growth and development in the K-12 years and their implications for program and curriculum development.

Bettie is a former Teacher-of-the-Year, Professor at San Diego State University, Executive Director of the Phoenix Foundation, and currently serves as a consultant to U.S. schools. She is the author of fourteen books that are published in twenty-three languages, as well as a number of popular audio cassette programs.

Dr. Youngs, a member of the National Speakers Association, addresses audiences throughout the U.S. and abroad, and meets with nearly 250,000 youth and adults each year. She serves on the Board of Directors for the National Council for Self-Esteem and is a frequent guest on radio and television talk shows. A leader in U.S. education, her consulting firm provides instruction and professional development to school districts nationwide. She may be contacted at:

Bettie B. Youngs & Associates
Instruction & Professional Development, Inc.
3060 Racetrack View Drive
Del Mar, CA 92014
(619) 481-6360

Here are more new books by author Bettie Youngs from Jalmar Press . . .

The 6 Vital Ingredients of Self-Esteem: How to Develop Them in Your Students
A Comprehensive Guide for K-12 Educators
Bettie B. Youngs, Ph.D., Ed.D.

Self-esteem is a consequence of six vital ingredients that empower or detract from the vitality of our lives. Written for educators, curriculum specialists, and childcare professionals, this comprehensive guide provides a thorough understanding of what self-esteem is and isn't, details how it is developed in the K-12 years, how educators develop or enhance it in students, and specifies skills and activities to help students develop a healthy self-concept to unleash potential and trigger the student's desire to excel and achieve.

"This valuable resource outlines a plan of action for building the six essential elements of self-esteem in the classroom and school environment. A must for every educator."
M. Dunaway, Ed.D., Secondary School Principal-of-the-Year

JP-9072-9   (208 pages) $19.95

Enhancing the Educator's Self-Esteem: It's Your Criteria #1
Bettie B. Youngs, Ph.D., Ed.D.

A healthy self-esteem is a prerequisite in being an effective educator; it's job criteria #1. Written for the educator *about* the educator, this comprehensive resource delineates ways in which the educator's self-esteem is positively or negatively charged in the school place by the nature of their work, and through interaction with students and colleagues. Discus-sion activities and exercises provide the educator with an opportunity to evaluate his or her educational philosophy, including skills for nourishing and rebuilding integrity toward personal value and a vital and healthy self-regard, and for [re]aligning professional respect.

"You're always taking care of your students, but who takes care of you? This book is about understanding and revitalizing our own sense of self. Every educator should have this important and personal handbook." ***Colleen Morey, Educator, Westin, Connecticut***

JP-9079-6   (144 pages) $16.95

You & Self-Esteem: Your Key to Happiness and Success
A Self-Esteem Workbook for Grades 5-12
Bettie B. Youngs, Ph.D., Ed.D.

This comprehensive and empowering resource written for young people, grades 5-12, helps them understand their "self-esteem" as well as the importance of a positive self-regard to being happy and good-natured, to being productive and achieving successful outcomes, to developing healthy and mutual friendships, and to provide skills to help young people themselves learn how to value, respect, and protect their own sense of self and well-being. This workbook is designed to be used as a supplementary resource or as a complete self-esteem course. Exercises and suggested writing assignments contained in each unit.

"This book is a complete guide for the young person on how to nourish and sustain a healthy self-esteem. Every student should have this book as a course."
Janet Dutrey, Educator, San Diego, California

JP-9083-4   (160 pages) $14.95

Other Works By Bettie B. Youngs, Ph.D.

BOOKS:

Stress in Children (New York: Avon Books, 1985)

Helping Your Teenager Deal With Stress (New York: Tarcher/St. Martins Press, 1986)

Is Your Net-Working? A Complete Guide to Building Contacts and Career Visibility
(New York: John Wiley & Sons, 1989)

Friendship Is Forever, Isn't It? (Rolling Hills Estates, CA: Jalmar Press, 1990)

Getting Back Together: Creating a New Relationship With Your Partner & Making It Last
(New York: Bob Adams, Inc., 1990)

The 6 Vital Ingredients of Self-Esteem: How to Develop Them in Your Child
(New York: Macmillan/Rawson, 1991)

A Stress Management Guide for Young People (Rolling Hills Estates, CA: Jalmar Press,
second edition, 1992)

Enhancing Educator's Self-Esteem: It's Your Criteria #1 (Rolling Hills Estates, CA: Jalmar
Press, 1992)

Problem Solving Skills For Children (Rolling Hills Estates, CA: Jalmar Press, second edition,
1992)

The 6 Vital Ingredients of Self-Esteem: How to Develop Them in Your Students
(Rolling Hills Estates, CA: Jalmar Press, 1992)

**You & Self-Esteem: It's The Key to Happiness & Success (A Self-Esteem Workbook for
Grades 5-12)** (Rolling Hills Estates, CA: Jalmar Press, 1992)

Stress Management for Administrators (Rolling Hills Estates, CA: Jalmar Press, 1993)

Goal Setting Skills for Young Adults (Rolling Hills Estates, CA: Jalmar Press, second edition,
1993)

The Teenager: A Guide to the Adolescent Years (Deerfield Beach, Florida: Health
Communications, 1993)

AUDIO CASSETTES:

Helping Your Teenager Deal With Stress (Deerfield Beach, Florida: Health Communications,
1993)

How to Raise Happy, Healthy, Self-Confident Children (Nightengale/Conant, 1990)

The 6 Vital Components of Self-Esteem and How to Develop Them in Your Child
(Sybervision, 1990)

Helping Children Manage Anxiety, Pressure, and Stress (Sybervision, 1991)

Developing Responsibility in Children (Sybervision, 1991)

Getting Back Together (Sybervision, 1991)

Table of Contents

INTRODUCTION

Virtually no one feels free of stress these days, certainly not classroom educators with too much to do and too little time to do it. Because you are working with too many students, some with special learning needs — be it gifted or limited — many with very complex emotional needs, hardly a day goes by when you are not stretched to capacity. In fact, in the corner of your mind that is not preoccupied with making sure Randy is not pummeling Bruce, Faye is doing her own work, wondering how you're going to coordinate calling Jena Johnson's mother — a traveling executive, and Tom Wassman's mother — who turned the reins for his whereabouts (and his education) over to her son long ago, and if Dr. Peters has gotten your latest request for a classroom aide, you may be thinking even now, "Do I *really* have the time to read this material?" In today's educational arena, stress seems to be an accepted facet of the professional's life, an "occupational hazard." That does not mean, however, that you must accept and suffer the resulting mental anguish and physical consequences stress can produce.

As educators, you're not alone in worrying about the demands of your work and the toll stress takes. A lot of time, expense, and effort is expended in recruiting competent, dedicated, and motivated educators. Administrators, too, want to know: How can we safeguard educators from the all too common enemy, stress? What can be done to stress-proof educators?

How much do you know about stress? How does it affect you and those around you? What is stress? What causes it? What can be done to manage stress, to moderate its negative effects? Can stress be used to your advantage? What stress management skills do you need? Given the nature of work in the classroom, how can educators continue to be effective day after day,

year after year, and remain at peak performance? Learning how to minimize your stress can help you perform your work with greater effectiveness. Learning how to manage your stress can also help you protect your health and well-being. This guide is designed to help you:

■ Examine the nature of stress and its impact on you, your classroom and school environment, your students, and your productivity.

■ Identify physical, emotional, and behavioral manifestations of stress and determine how you respond to stress.

■ Delineate factors in the schoolplace that commonly produce stress, and ways to minimize their negative aspects.

■ Learn key intervention and prevention strategies to manage stress.

Each of us responds in different ways to stress-producing factors. How violently or calmly you respond to stress itself is under your control. Many professionally effective and personally powerful people, recognizing that the power to do so lies within themselves, are able to manage stress competently and turn it to their advantage. The question then is not whether to eliminate stress altogether (a difficult if not impossible goal), but how to manage it — or rather, manage our *response* to it. Once you know what causes you stress and how you respond to it, you'll be better able to develop skills and strategies for minimizing and managing it.

Because each of us interprets and assigns different meaning (power) to stress-producing events, there is no ready-made, "de-stress" formula that can accommodate everyone. Managing stress is a personal agenda; it means minimizing those situations that have the potential to produce stress and managing yourself in

1

stressful situations that are unavoidable. But there is a format — a pattern, so to speak — upon which we can all tailor our approach. It consists of working through four identifiable phases:

- **Phase I:** Understanding stress and its manifestations.

- **Phase II:** Identifying individual factors that provide stress for you and recognizing how you respond to those stressors.

- **Phase III:** Identifying and implementing coping strategies to reduce those stressors.

- **Phase IV:** Making a commitment to prioritize your well-being and effectively manage your stress.

Since you can't avoid all stress, the goal becomes to disarm its negative effects and the toll it exacts from you. You must manage it so as not to endanger your own health and productivity as well as that of your students and colleagues. Your overall goal is to use stress constructively to promote health, self-development, and productivity.

HOW TO USE THIS MANUAL

How much you get out of this manual depends primarily on how well you *use* it. The first key is *availability*. Don't put this on your bookshelf at home. Keep this copy handy, perhaps in your desk drawer, in your briefcase, or with those few key books sitting on the corner of your desk. Refer to it often: Set aside time each week to examine and evaluate how you're doing. Are you managing well? Are you handling stress successfully? What stressors keep you from attaining peak performance and teaching excellence and from experiencing personal joy and satisfaction in your work?

A second key to gleaning the most from this manual is *practice*. Go through the materials frequently because you and your needs are always changing. For example, the students who drove you crazy yesterday show up today with big grins and correctly completed homework . . . but the teacher next door suddenly decides to let her students do their project in the hall, creating noise and a lack of attention on the part of your own students who would like to be out there too. You may find that you have a new frame of reference when you read the material a second or a third time. To help you with the practice portion, multiple copies of the worksheets are available in each section. Complete a worksheet, then a few days or a week later, do a second copy of the same worksheet and compare the two to see your progress.

A third essential element if you intend to benefit from this manual is *application*. Mitigating stress is not a nebulous idea. Stress exacts a toll — there's a price to be paid for the stress that isn't channeled effectively, and there are repercussions. Learn the theories and ideas given in this manual, then take the time to APPLY the techniques discussed. It's all too easy to read something and think, "That sounds good; I should do that sometime," and continue on in the same manner as before. As you know, learning is best achieved through practice and application. So keep this manual *available, practice* the exercises frequently, and *apply* the information daily. By doing so, you make this manual a helpful and purposeful tool.

WHAT IS STRESS?

The Cue to Adapt and Make a Change

Very simply, stress is the name given to the reaction of the body mobilizing its defenses against any perceived threat. Stress is the body's physical, mental and chemical reaction to circumstances that cause confusion, irritation, or excitement. It results not so much from the stress-producing event itself, but rather, from the way you perceive and handle (process) that event — therefore, stress can have either a positive or negative charge. In other words, the perception of stress is under *your* control.

How you manage stressful events is up to you. Handled poorly, stress becomes an enemy which debilitates you; at its extreme, it contributes to weakening the body, making it less able to ward off diseases. Handled well, it can signal the brain to release more fuel, providing extra strength to meet an immediate circumstance, and it can strengthen you for the next encounter. Some stress reactions are so subdued that you're not even aware of them. Others show themselves clearly in tension, heart palpitations, inability to concentrate, insomnia, headaches, muscle tension, even ulcers. Short-term stress can cause symptoms like severe headaches and stomachaches. Excessive stress on a long-term basis can cause ulcers and trigger diseases such as high blood pressure and arthritis. Unbridled stress can contribute to heart disease and the weakening of body organs. Stress produces a chain reaction, whether positive and negative, that is chemical/physical as well as mental.

In a very real sense the stress response is a cue to cope, to adapt, to make a change, and to prepare you to take action. In stressful situations, messages from the brain, acting through the hypothalamus, stimulate the sympathetic nerves and the pituitary thereby triggering an outpouring of adrenaline from the adrenal glands. Circulation speeds up, more energy-rich sugar appears in the blood, muscles tense, saliva decreases, eyes dilate, senses become more acute, the thyroid is activated, and the body's muscle function is strengthened. At the same time, blood cells are released from storage depots into the circulation and the digestive system goes into temporary inaction. All of these reactions are designed to help the body gear up for action. When the stress situation eases, this reaction shuts down. However, in periods of prolonged stress this automatic mechanism can become exhausted, making a person more susceptible to illness.

THE BIOLOGY OF STRESS

The notion that stress is just in the mind is simply not accurate. A first step toward understanding what stress is, how it translates into human suffering, how it can be reduced, and how we can effectively and productively manage it, is to look at stress as a biological occurrence.

Most people think of stress as the daily demands of life. Technically, these demands are called "stressors" and the actual wear and tear on our body is "stress." The stressor may be a biochemical insult (a glass of wine you feel entitled to after a hard day of trying to explain to students just why they have to know the leading exports of Botswana); it may be a physical injury (if only you could be sure that it was an accident when Bobby let the door slam on your foot!); or it may be an emotional arousal (fear of being laid off during teacher cutbacks, irritation at not having enough materials to do your job thoroughly, or pride and satisfaction when a student takes the time to tell you what you mean to her). Whatever the source, the mind and body issue a response, resulting in three interrelated phases: (1) the alarm reaction, (2) resistance/adaptation, and (3) exhaustion/burnout. Let's examine each phase more closely.

The Alarm Reaction

The alarm reaction phase alerts the body that it is undergoing a stress *reaction*. Perhaps you have heard this referred to as the "fight or flight response." The body is notified to act, and a series of events occur to help it do so. You may recognize from your own experience some of the alarm reaction responses initiated by the autonomic nervous system.

1. Have you ever had a "nervous stomach?" Because it is more important to be alert and strong in the face of danger than to digest food, digestion slows so that blood may be directed to the muscles and the brain.

2. Can you remember trying to catch your breath after being anxious? Breathing gets faster to supply more oxygen to the muscles.

3. Do you recall how your heart pounded when that speeding car wheeled around the corner and just missed you? The heart speeds up and blood pressure soars, forcing blood to parts of the body that need to take action.

4. Do you use extra deodorant on the day you're scheduled to go over your performance review with your building administrator or curriculum director? Perspiration increases to cool the body. This in turn allows the body to burn more energy.

5. Do you ever complain of a stiff neck or of chest pain after a stressful day? Muscles tense in preparation for important action and stay tense when under stress.

6. Have you noticed how quickly some wounds stop bleeding? Chemicals are released to make the blood clot more rapidly. If you are injured, this clotting can reduce blood loss.

7. Were you ever surprised by your quickness, alertness, and seemingly extra strength and endurance during an emergency? Remember getting your "second wind?" Sugars and fats pour into the bloodstream to provide fuel for quick energy.

Resistance/Adaptation

Within moments after you perceive the stressor (your response to the situation or event), the secondary phase of this process, called the General Adaptation Syndrome, goes into full swing (shown in Illustration #1 on page 5). Almost immediately, and in direct relationship to the diminishing of an exterior threat, the body attempts to return biochemically to its normal balance (homeostasis). This resistance stage essentially reverses the biochemical processes described earlier in the alarm stage. The body attempts to adapt itself to a state of calm and tranquility by re-lowering blood pressure, heart rate, respiration, and core body temperature.

In many ways adaptation is the critical stage. If the perceived stressor has disappeared or been overcome, the body tries to reverse the alarm reaction. However, if the exposure to the stressor continues, the body will replace those emergency bodily changes with adaptive ones. Certain bodily reactions then become fixed. For example, muscles will remain tense long after the stressor has disappeared. A great deal of energy and vital resources are required for this kind of resistance, and in the process essential minerals and vitamins necessary for healthy functioning are depleted.

ILLUSTRATION #1

General Adaptation Syndrome

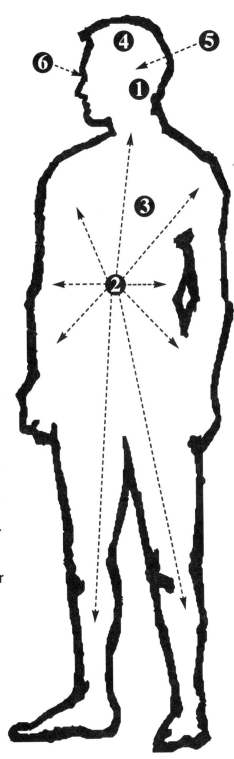

❶

A small portion of the brain called the hypothalmus has triggered the pituitary gland, located near the base of the brain, and now its hormone, ACTH, is released into your bloodstream.

❷

ACTH goes directly to the adrenal glands, which then step up their output of adrenaline into your bloodstream, along with related hormones called corticoids. These hormones bring your body up to its aroused state.

Within the first eight seconds, the bloodstream has carried these stress organizers into every cell in your body.

At the same time, commands are traveling through the nerve communication system to alert heart, lungs, and muscles for action. The muscles have been more richly supplied with blood, as the tiny vessels constrict and your blood pressure increases. However, blood has been diverted away from your extremities. The liver, too, is working harder to convert its stored glycogen into glucose which the brain and muscles will need in greater supply.

❸

Meanwhile, your breathing is more rapid, increasing the amount of oxygen in the blood, which enables the muscles and the brain to burn that glucose more efficiently.

Your heart is pumping away, sending an abundant supply of blood to the priority portions of the body. Your skeletal muscles brace, and, with the blood you need in your stomach reduced in favor of those high priority areas elsewhere, you're going to have indigestion. Over time, this can develop into ulcers.

❹

Now your brain is busy with preparations for violent physical action — one reason why you can't think very effectively on abstract levels during this panic state.

❺

On the other hand, your hearing may become more acute.

❻

The pupils of your eyes dilate, making your vision sensitive.

Exhaustion/Burnout

When a period of stress is prolonged, the adaptive mechanisms are eventually depleted and the body enters the exhaustion stage. Stress experts believe that exhaustion sets in when the body undergoes an intense stress response lasting beyond six to eight weeks. As a result the body tires and loses its coping resilience. This biochemical exhaustion is sometimes referred to as "burnout."

If the stressor continues to present itself as a threat to the body or is repeated (or if other stressors follow at close intervals), the energy required for this kind of adaptation is gone. Wear and tear results in the so-called "diseases of adaptation." Have you ever noticed, for example, how quickly you catch a cold or the flu when your resistance is low and how long it seems to linger? The ability to withstand stress has been diminished. The longer the tension continues, the greater the damage may be to your body.

Pathological Stress

Stress becomes pathological when your body reacts as though it's still in the alarm phase long after the actual threat has passed. For example, elevated blood pressure under stress is a normal reaction, but when it persists it becomes hypertension; heart-rate acceleration, if prolonged, is diagnosed as tachycardia; and a normal blood shift away from the stomach, if it continues beyond the period of stress, becomes a loss of appetite.

SCIENCE OF THE MIND: THE PSYCHOLOGY OF STRESS

When an individual is forced to adapt or readjust to an event, reactions occur in both the mind and the body. Why some individuals become ill and others do not under the same stressful conditions is determined to a great extent by the individual's interpretation of the stressor. You don't get an ulcer by standing out in the rain or sun too long. An ulcer is a symptom, a sign, that you are not coping well with whatever it is that's disturbing to you.

When normal stress reactions are prolonged and unabated, a psychosomatic illness is likely to develop. Depression is a prime example. On a behavioral level we see people under prolonged stress using tranquilizers, drinking more heavily than they might normally, or getting into harmful patterns of overeating and smoking. Constant pressure can cause unhealthy behavior, such as the negative effects of Type A behavior. Stress elicits physiological, psychological, and behavioral symptoms simultaneously.

Prolonged Stress = Burnout = Emotional and Physical Dropout

Exhaustion contributes to burnout. This in turn can lead to emotional or physical withdrawal. There may be a noticeable loss of the interest, thoroughness, and vitality you once brought to your work. You may care less about what others think of you or how they perceive your effectiveness; you may lose interest in your appearance; you may tolerate your sagging self-esteem without seeking active ways to refuel it, or neglect to value your personhood and hold it in the highest esteem, thereby starting a downward spiral of dysfunctional or even destructive behaviors; you may stop caring about and helping others; you may lose interest in those things you once greatly enjoyed — hobbies, sports, reading, and so on. You may experience a feeling of apathy or a general level of lingering frustration.

If you continue to experience debilitating feelings (frustration, anger, sadness, hopelessness), you may become less exuberant and vital in the way you live your life. Feeling overwhelmed and unable to cope can cause you to drop out. This may be physical — you are frequently absent or you actually quit your job. Or it can be psychological — you start a cycle of "get-by" performance in your teaching, assign more busywork to keep the students quiet, let your aide take over more and more, or (a favorite last resort!) show more films — basically abandoning the function of interacting in the teaching/learning experience.

The toll your stress exacts doesn't just affect you. Its repercussions often contribute to the stress levels of those around you. Studies on the effects of stress on teachers' behaviors, for example, show that educators who are under stress (real or perceived) cause great amounts of stress for their students: Not only do these teachers give their students fewer positive reinforcements (the most effective way to change human behavior) but they give out more negative reinforcements. They also resort to negative ways of controlling and managing student behavior.

If you're not adept at dealing with stress effectively and most especially if you avoid confronting it, you may stockpile hurts, letting them build up to intolerable levels. Eventually, you lose your idealism, the drive and motivation that led to your being entrusted with a position as an educator; you are no longer passionate about your work and your call to teach. You in effect betray those who believe in you, those who felt you capable of helping others.

Warning Signs of Stress

Stress shows itself in three ways: physically, emotionally, and behaviorally. Some of the common symptoms of stress are listed below. Learn to recognize these symptoms early and heed their warnings.

- Headaches
- Nervousness
- Inability to get rid of bad thoughts (or recurring bad dreams)
- Faintness or dizziness
- Loss of sexual interest

- Excessive criticism of others
- Difficulty in speaking when you are excited
- Continual feelings of annoyance and irritation
- Pains in the heart or chest
- Low energy or bouts of high energy followed by depression
- Excessive perspiration
- Poor appetite/excessive appetite
- Feeling like a victim, of being trapped with no way out of the situation
- Outbursts of temper you cannot control
- Pains in the lower part of your back
- Frequently "blue," lonely feelings
- Lack of interest in things once enjoyed
- Constant fearfulness
- Easily hurt feelings
- Suspiciousness
- Feeling that others do not understand you or are unsympathetic
- Feeling that people are unfriendly or dislike you
- Heart pounding or racing
- Lowered self-esteem
- Nausea or upset stomach
- Inferiority feelings
- Sleep difficulties (too much/too little)
- Difficulty making decisions
- Continual feelings of wanting to be alone
- Trouble getting your breath
- Loss of concentration
- Hopeless feelings about the future
- Trouble concentrating
- Weakness in parts of your body

STRESS: AN INDIVIDUAL MATTER

The concept of stress means something different to each of us. The business person may think of it as frustration or emotional tension, the airtraffic controller as a problem in concentration, the biochemist as a purely chemical event, the athlete as muscular tension, the parent as an overwhelming and demanding schedule, the small child as a stomachache. You, the classroom educator, may think of it as a discipline problem with a fractious student or a demanding or irate parent, the frustration of having too much paperwork or having more to do with less resources due to declining budgets, or something else entirely. While stress is no more than anxiety or physical nervousness to some individuals, in others it can lead to emotional despair. What is stressful for someone else may not be to you, and vice versa.

Why Is Being an Educator So Stressful?

Did you know that next to air traffic controllers, teaching is rated as the next most stressful occupation? You probably did! There are a multitude of reasons why educators are experiencing stress and anxiety in alarming proportions. Educators often say they feel isolated and have little opportunity to interact with their colleagues. They sometimes feel physically cut off from other adults in a room filled only with students, and they long for the emotional support of others who have faced similar situations. Other reasons have to do with student apathy, inadequate preparation time and not enough support from superiors. Some educators say that parents are less interested in their children's school and education than they used to be, that they sometimes feel alone in their concerns for assisting students in learning. The reasons are numerous and differ from school to school, from educator to educator, from situation to situation, and even from day to day. Cristina, an elementary school teacher from the Denver Public School System, described a recent stressful day this way:

"If I were a machine, my red lights would have been flashing and my buzzers and alarms all sounding last Thursday. The music teacher

was out with the flu. That meant that I didn't get the 45 minutes away from my students that her presence brings. I always look forward to that time when I can catch up on some paperwork. The first thing I saw when I got in this morning was the note that she would be absent; what a bad way to start the day. The students wanted a music lesson, though, so I had to do my best, leading them in a singalong that was loud and enthusiastic, but more noise than music. Neighboring teachers complained about it.

"Everyone in the school has a short temper because of teacher contract negotiations. There was an atmosphere of 'us vs. them' in the halls and lounge, with teachers and administrators at odds. I really dislike that because one of my favorite things about our school is the warmth and comradery. One of my students showed up with bruises on her arms again, making me more convinced than ever that she is an abused child.

"Then in the middle of all these problems a personal one arose. My husband called and said that he really needed a three-day weekend. He wanted me to cut school tomorrow. When I told him I just couldn't, he became upset. He took out his frustration on me by mocking what he calls my 'irreplaceable fixation.' He taunted me with, 'You think that if your students had to have a substitute for even one day, their educational processes would be short-circuited. If you would take some of your accumulated sick days, we could have a life outside of your work.' I had too much work to do, a tense, overcharged atmosphere to do it in, frustration and sadness over the problems of a helpless child, and now a cross between guilt and anger at my own personal situation. Last Thursday was a day I just could have done without."

If Cristina had more than a month of "Thursdays" in a row, her chances for burnout would be great. Chances are she would think more about how frustrated she was and less about how to overcome the frustration. Avoidance behavior might follow. For example, she might not return her husband's calls in order not to deal with the added conflict, thus refusing to create a win-win decision. Or she might take less of an interest in detail, not spending as much time with students, not adequately preparing for class, and so on.

Notice in Illustration #2 on page 10, how short-term, negative coping can lead to long-term problems, while effective intervention can lead to positive outcomes.

Perhaps you would have responded differently in Cristina's position. Stress is an individual interpretation. Think about a recent stressful experience in your life. In the space below describe it. It could be a dispute with your building administrator, a philosophical difference with a fellow teacher, a personality conflict with a student, a dispute with a parent, or any of a number of events. What's the big stressor for you right now?

A big stressor for me right now is:

_____

_____

_____

_____

_____

_____

Now think about how you were affected by that stress. How did you react? Before you list yours, let's look at how Cristina identified her stress responses:

Physical Signs

I felt nauseated.

I had a headache.

I lost my appetite.

I felt dizzy.

Emotional Signs

I felt like crying.

I was angry.

I felt trapped in a no-win situation.

I found it difficult to block out angry feelings toward my husband's lack of understanding; these thoughts dominated the remainder of my day.

Behavioral Signs

I felt scattered and unsure about the quality of my teaching.

I was impatient with my students and other teachers.

I wasn't outgoing, friendly, and supportive.

In the categories below, list your reactions to the stress you're dealing with now.

Physical Signs

_____

_____

_____

_____

Emotional Signs

_____

_____

_____

Behavioral Signs

_____

_____

_____

_____

Illustration #2

THE TWO STRESS CYCLES:
DISTRESS AND WELLNESS

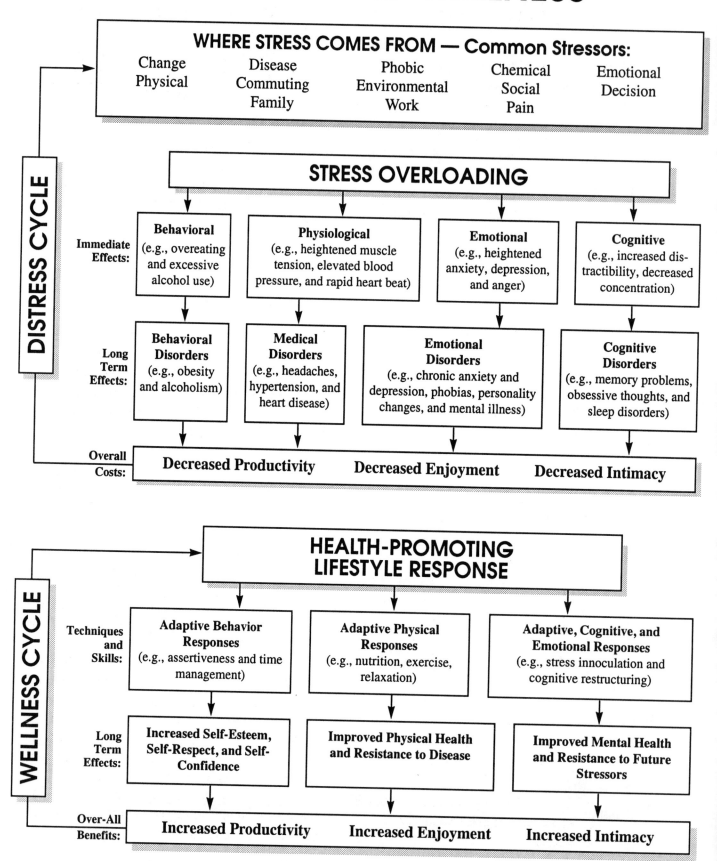

WHERE STRESS COMES FROM — Common Stressors:

Change	Disease	Phobic	Chemical	Emotional
Physical	Commuting	Environmental	Social	Decision
	Family	Work	Pain	

DISTRESS CYCLE

STRESS OVERLOADING

Immediate Effects:

Behavioral (e.g., overeating and excessive alcohol use)

Physiological (e.g., heightened muscle tension, elevated blood pressure, and rapid heart beat)

Emotional (e.g., heightened anxiety, depression, and anger)

Cognitive (e.g., increased distractibility, decreased concentration)

Long Term Effects:

Behavioral Disorders (e.g., obesity and alcoholism)

Medical Disorders (e.g., headaches, hypertension, and heart disease)

Emotional Disorders (e.g., chronic anxiety and depression, phobias, personality changes, and mental illness)

Cognitive Disorders (e.g., memory problems, obsessive thoughts, and sleep disorders)

Overall Costs:

Decreased Productivity   **Decreased Enjoyment**   **Decreased Intimacy**

HEALTH-PROMOTING LIFESTYLE RESPONSE

WELLNESS CYCLE

Techniques and Skills:

Adaptive Behavior Responses (e.g., assertiveness and time management)

Adaptive Physical Responses (e.g., nutrition, exercise, relaxation)

Adaptive, Cognitive, and Emotional Responses (e.g., stress innoculation and cognitive restructuring)

Long Term Effects:

Increased Self-Esteem, Self-Respect, and Self-Confidence

Improved Physical Health and Resistance to Disease

Improved Mental Health and Resistance to Future Stressors

Over-All Benefits:

Increased Productivity   **Increased Enjoyment**   **Increased Intimacy**

ARE YOU A STRESS SEEKER?

I've said that stress is unique to the individual. We each respond to the event differently: Not everyone wants to avoid it. In fact, there are those who actually look for stress, who thrive under pressure! Maybe you wait until a deadline is approaching before you begin a task, thereby creating a pressure for yourself to complete it on time. If that's your style, it could be that you're a stress seeker. The following checklist will help you decide. Rate yourself as to how you typically react in each of the situations listed. Use a rating of 4 to mean "Always," 3 to mean "Frequently," 2 to mean "Sometimes," and 1 to mean "Never."

Are You a Stress Seeker?

____ 1. Do you have a tendency to put things off until the last minute and then frantically rush to get them done?

____ 2. Do you thrive on situations in which there is pressure, competition, tension, or risk?

____ 3. Do you find stress or tension has been a driving force behind many of your major accomplishments?

____ 4. Do you feel exhilarated or energized after accomplishing a difficult task or closing an important business deal?

____ 5. Do you enjoy novelty and challenge in your work?

____ 6. Do you have a tendency to see obstacles as challenges rather than headaches?

____ 7. Are you constantly seeking ways to improve yourself or your performance in your field?

____ 8. In general, would you classify yourself as a risk taker rather than a risk avoider?

____ 9. Are you willing to give up job security for job challenge?

____10. Are you able to "come down" physically and emotionally a few hours after a tension-producing event?

____11. Do you seek action-oriented vacations?

____12. In your leisure time, do you pursue activities in which there is a certain amount of danger or risk, for example, skydiving, rock climbing?

ANALYSIS: What does your total score mean? If your score is between 36 and 48, you are a true stress seeker who enjoys excitement and exhilaration. You actually look around for and create a high stress level to propel you to action. You like stress. You *thrive* on it! If your score is between 24 and 35, you probably like things to go smoothly; you like harmony and strive to keep things in perspective, to balance your life in order to stay on an even keel. A score between 12 and 23 indicates that you are likely to avoid stress and seek security instead. You don't like to be charged with emotion and find such conditions drain and sap your energy.

Information about how you respond to stress can provide you with insight into the age levels of students you enjoy working with the most. It also reveals the reason why you prefer to organize your room as you do, gives rise to the rules and consequences you set for student behavior (and clues as to how you'll deal with student behavior), and sheds light on your style of teaching. Are you comfortable when your students are divided into small groups and carry on discussions, for example, or do you prefer that your students work on their own with paper and pencil activities, raising a hand when they have a question or need to seek clarification? Are your students sitting anywhere they like, or are they in assigned seats?

CHARTING YOUR STRESS

Did you catch yourself becoming alarmed when reading the list of stress-related symptoms because you felt you have all or most of them? Relax. Everyone has those symptoms at one time or another. It's when the symptoms become too common and too frequent that you need to be concerned. Just when is that? How will you know when the stress level is too much? One way is to *check for frequency and intensity of the stress symptoms*. For example, you may be a little nervous or suspicious on occasion, but when you find yourself always nervous or suspicious, it's time to take action. Of course, in order to identify what is out of the ordinary, you must first realize what is normal for you. The Daily Stress Log worksheet at the end of this section can help you monitor your daily reaction to stress and to related stress symptoms. Here's how to use it.

Instructions for Keeping a Daily Log

Whenever you develop a stress-related symptom, such as a headache or muscular tension, place a mark in the Daily Log above the time of day the symptom began and estimate the approximate intensity level of the symptom. Rate the intensity of the pain or discomfort on a scale of 1 (very weak intensity) to 10 (very high intensity). Indicate the different intensity levels of the symptom from hour to hour throughout the day, connecting each intensity mark to the next hour's mark with a straight line so as to make a line graph. Label each line graph according to the symptom it records. In the event that you experience a high-intensity but short-lived symptom, place a mark above the time it occurred at the approximate intensity level and label the mark with its corresponding symptom. Dizziness or quickened heart rate are examples of short-duration symptoms.

Stress symptoms interfere to different degrees with our abilities to function, depending on the intensity of the stress symptom. Indicate in parentheses next to each time and intensity-level mark the extent to which the symptom's presence interferes with your ongoing activity. On a scale of 1 to 100, 1 represents no interference whatsoever and 100 means total incapacity. Consider such things as your attention and concentration, memory, capacity to learn new information, decision-making ability, logic, effectiveness of time utilization, ability to interact effectively and comfortably with others, and job and overall performance. Indicate what you were doing when the symptom interfered.

At the top of the Daily Stress Log indicate how many hours you engage in work-related activities, whether at school or at home. Next, estimate the percentage of on-the-job time you spend in interpersonal work, when others depend directly and immediately upon your performance.

You'll find eight specific categories below the graph. Here's what they mean.

1. *Accomplishments:* List what you did that day, for example, finally got Susie to check out a library book; talked to Enrique's parents; revised lesson plan; met with music teacher.

2. *Unfinished Business:* Show what you did not get done today, for example, peer evaluation forms; meeting with vice-principal regarding extracurricular duties.

3. *Excuses and Avoidance Strategies:* Cite the reasons you gave yourself as rationalizations for not doing the tasks; list the things you did to *postpone* doing the tasks, for example, cleaned out a desk drawer instead of making an unpleasant phone call.

4. *Instances of Tension:* List those times you noticed you were especially tense, when you caught yourself clenching your fists.

5. *Relaxation Techniques:* What did you do to calm down; did you take a walk, chat with a friend?

6. *Alcoholic Beverages:* Note the type and quantity.

7. *Cigarettes Smoked:* List the number (be sure to include those you "bummed" from someone else; they count too!).

8. *Medications:* Did you take aspirin or a prescription drug? Note the name and dosage.

Interpretation of Cristina's Log

Look at the copy of Cristina's Daily Stress Log. Let's analyze just one of the factors in Cristina's chart as an example. It's obvious that her stress begins a couple of hours into the morning and builds. A headache started at 10:00 a.m. and worsened over the next hour. By noon Cristina was frowning and tense. Just before going to lunch, she noted that she was extremely short-tempered. Coming back from lunch, she was fine until almost the end of the the day when she became anxious again.

How can Cristina interpret this factor? She realizes that some of her stress is tied to (mal)nutrition. When she first comes in, she's fine. As the morning and her hunger builds (she does not eat a breakfast), she becomes headachy and irritable. She is especially sluggish just before lunch. After lunch she is fine for a few hours, then becomes nervous again. She is keyed up before dinner at home, but has no significant signs of stress after dinner.

What possible solutions can Cristina come up with? If she notices over time that regardless of her activities, she still follows this same general pattern, she might decide to eat a breakfast, have a mid-morning snack, or mini-meals in the course of a day. A glass of milk or piece of fruit might work. Cristina skips breakfast and eats lunch rather late in the day. If she's at school by 7:00 a.m. and doesn't get to lunch until 12:50 p.m., she is probably overly hungry. Note also that Cristina's teaching schedule is such that her most demanding courses are in the morning, before lunch. In this one area, then, she will need to find creative ways to make changes.

The value of a chart like this is to get a *picture* of when your stress occurs and how severe it is. Two copies of the Daily Stress Log are included to get you started. Make additional copies as needed. Once you have used the Daily Stress Log for a few days and acquainted yourself with it, it should take but a few moments of your time each day. Keep the log for seven consecutive days to get an overall picture of your general level of stress and your response to stress.

CRISTINA'S STRESS LOG

Date _____

If a workday, indicate (1) how many hours spent in relation to your job _____, and (2) estimate of percentage of on-the-job time spent interacting with others (teaching, meeting with other teachers, talking to parents, etc.).

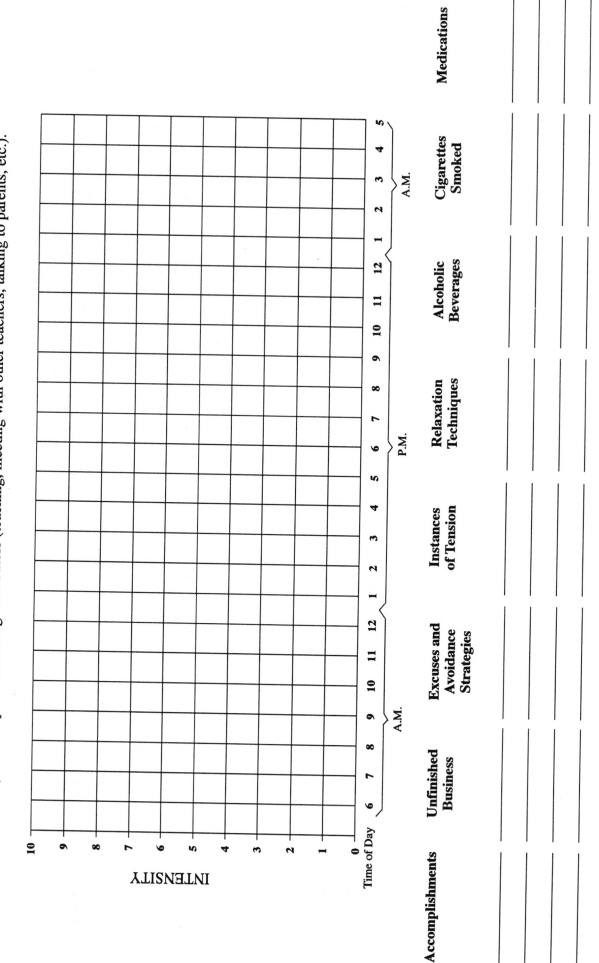

INTENSITY

Time of Day

| | | | | | | | | | | | | | | | | | | | | | | | | |
|6|7|8|9|10|11|12|1|2|3|4|5|6|7|8|9|10|11|12|1|2|3|4|5|

A.M.   P.M.   A.M.

| Accomplishments | Unfinished Business | Excuses and Avoidance Strategies | Instances of Tension | Relaxation Techniques | Alcoholic Beverages | Cigarettes Smoked | Medications |

MONDAY STRESS LOG

Date _____

If a workday, indicate (1) how many hours spent in relation to your job _____, and (2) estimate of percentage of on-the-job time spent interacting with others (teaching, meeting with other teachers, talking to parents, etc.).

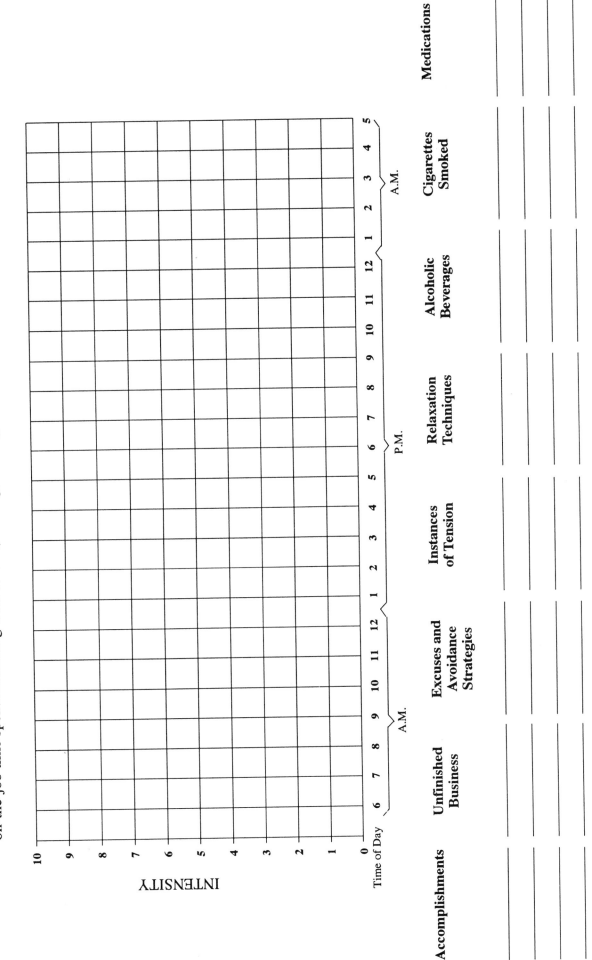

INTENSITY

Time of Day																							
6	7	8	9	10	11	12	1	2	3	4	5	6	7	8	9	10	11	12	1	2	3	4	5

A.M.   P.M.   A.M.

Accomplishments	Unfinished Business	Excuses and Avoidance Strategies	Instances of Tension	Relaxation Techniques	Alcoholic Beverages	Cigarettes Smoked	Medications

TUESDAY STRESS LOG

Date _____

If a workday, indicate (1) how many hours spent in relation to your job _____, and (2) estimate of percentage of on-the-job time spent interacting with others (teaching, meeting with other teachers, talking to parents, etc.).

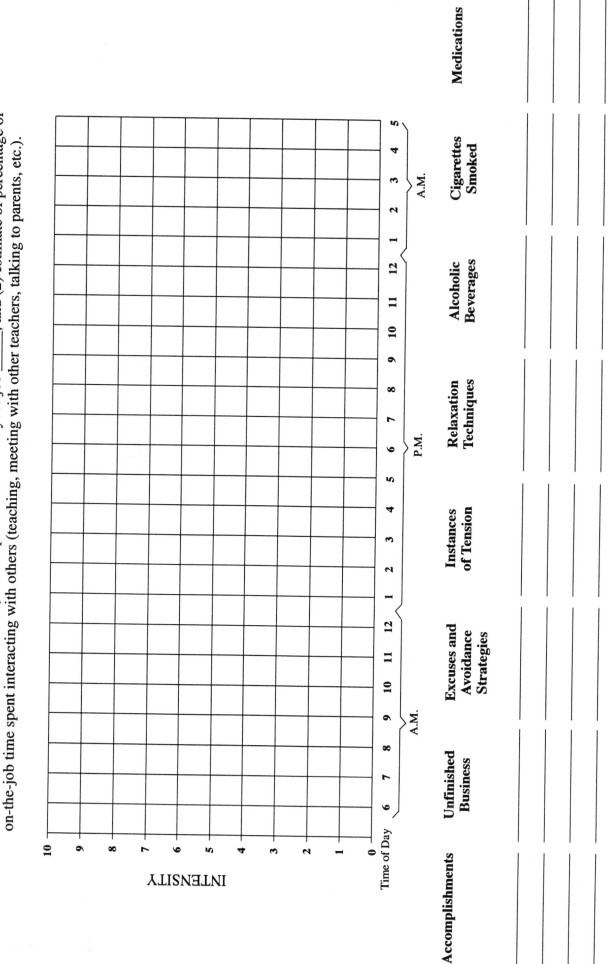

INTENSITY

Time of Day   6   7   8   9   10   11   12   1   2   3   4   5   6   7   8   9   10   11   12   1   2   3   4   5

A.M.   P.M.   A.M.

| Accomplishments | Unfinished Business | Excuses and Avoidance Strategies | Instances of Tension | Relaxation Techniques | Alcoholic Beverages | Cigarettes Smoked | Medications |

WEDNESDAY STRESS LOG

Date _____

If a workday, indicate (1) how many hours spent in relation to your job _____, and (2) estimate of percentage of on-the-job time spent interacting with others (teaching, meeting with other teachers, talking to parents, etc.).

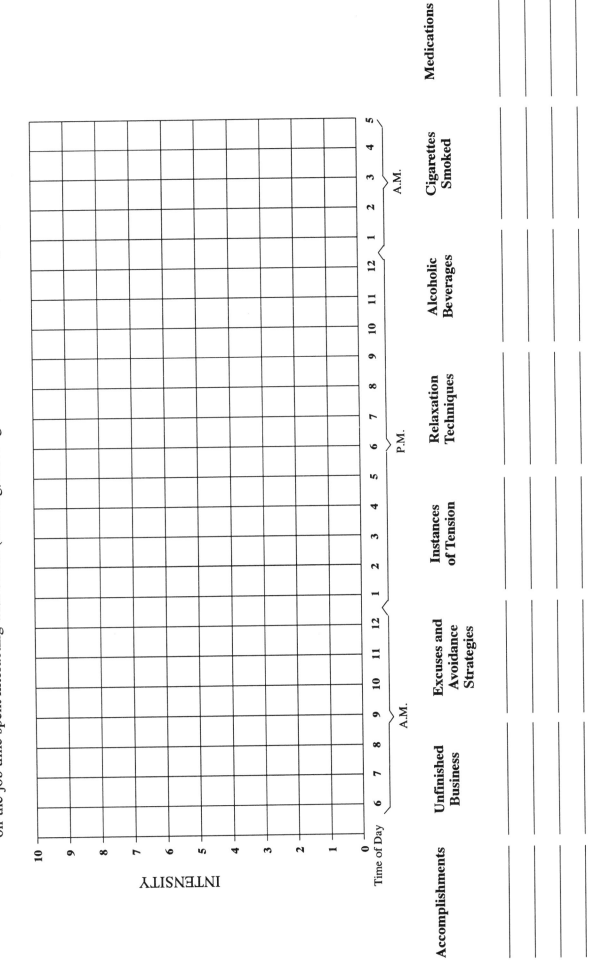

THURSDAY STRESS LOG

Date _____

If a workday, indicate (1) how many hours spent in relation to your job _____, and (2) estimate of percentage of on-the-job time spent interacting with others (teaching, meeting with other teachers, talking to parents, etc.).

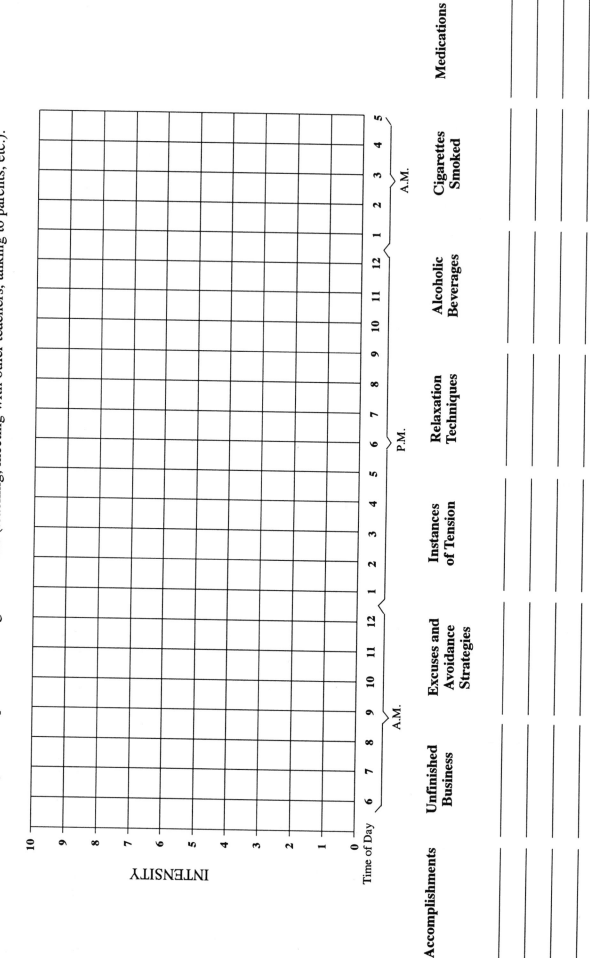

INTENSITY

10
9
8
7
6
5
4
3
2
1
0

Time of Day

6 7 8 9 10 11 12 1 2 3 4 5 6 7 8 9 10 11 12 1 2 3 4 5

A.M. P.M. A.M.

Accomplishments	Unfinished Business	Excuses and Avoidance Strategies	Instances of Tension	Relaxation Techniques	Alcoholic Beverages	Cigarettes Smoked	Medications

FRIDAY STRESS LOG

Date _____

If a workday, indicate (1) how many hours spent in relation to your job _____, and (2) estimate of percentage of on-the-job time spent interacting with others (teaching, meeting with other teachers, talking to parents, etc.).

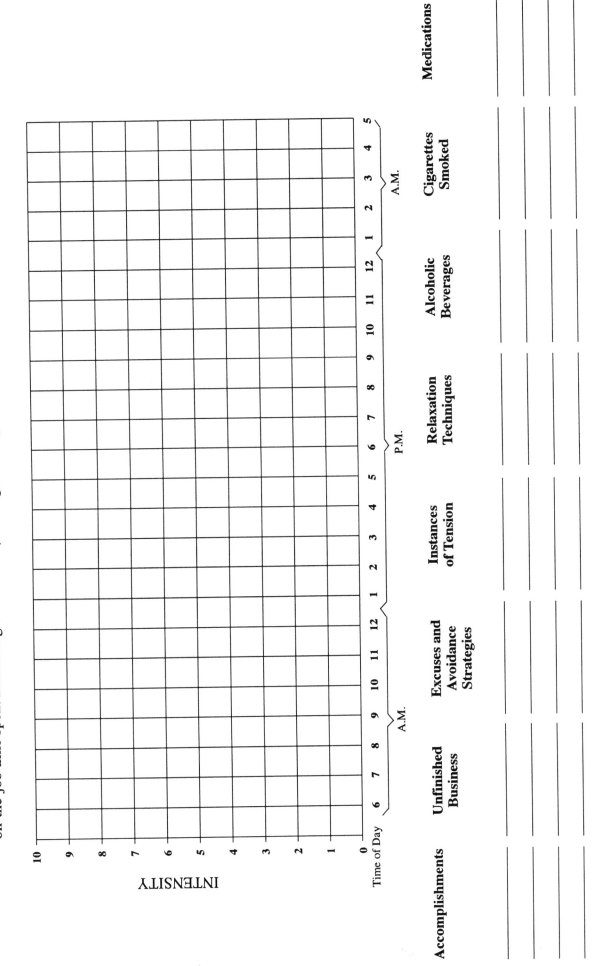

INTENSITY

10
9
8
7
6
5
4
3
2
1
0

Time of Day

6 7 8 9 10 11 12 1 2 3 4 5 6 7 8 9 10 11 12 1 2 3 4 5

A.M.   P.M.   A.M.

Unfinished Business	Excuses and Avoidance Strategies	Instances of Tension	Relaxation Techniques	Alcoholic Beverages	Cigarettes Smoked

Accomplishments

Medications

SATURDAY STRESS LOG

Date _____

If a workday, indicate (1) how many hours spent in relation to your job _____, and (2) estimate of percentage of on-the-job time spent interacting with others (teaching, meeting with other teachers, talking to parents, etc.).

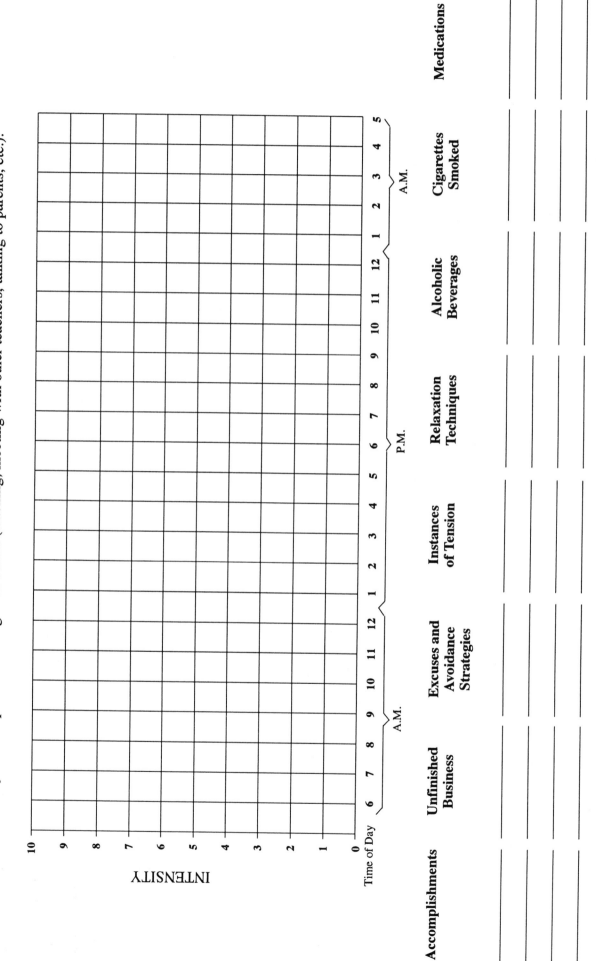

INTENSITY

10
9
8
7
6
5
4
3
2
1
0

Time of Day   6 7 8 9 10 11 12 1 2 3 4 5 6 7 8 9 10 11 12 1 2 3 4 5

A.M.   P.M.   A.M.

| Unfinished Business | Excuses and Avoidance Strategies | Instances of Tension | Relaxation Techniques | Alcoholic Beverages | Cigarettes Smoked | Medications |

Accomplishments

SUNDAY STRESS LOG

Date _____

If a workday, indicate (1) how many hours spent in relation to your job _____, and (2) estimate of percentage of on-the-job time spent interacting with others (teaching, meeting with other teachers, talking to parents, etc.).

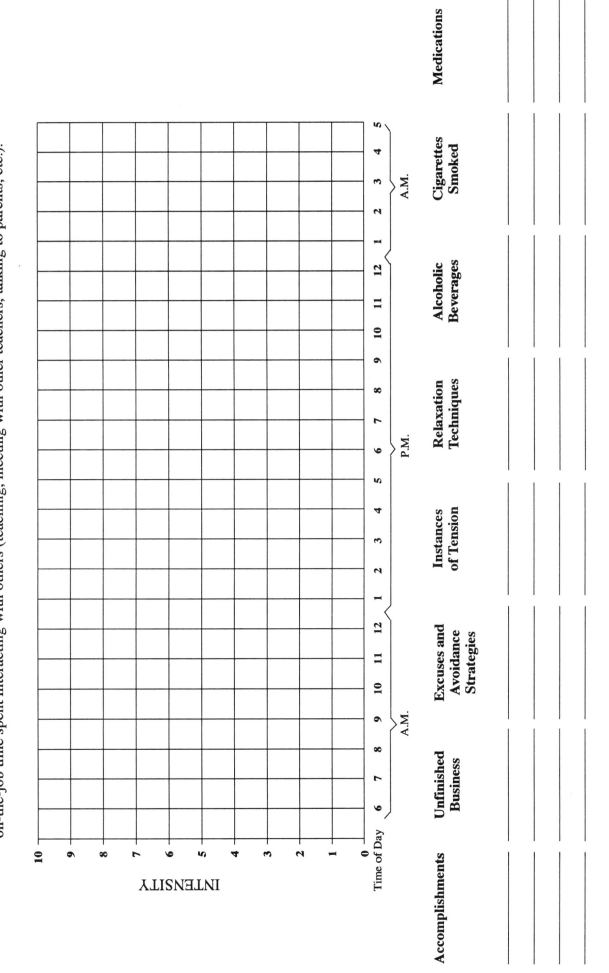

Accomplishments | Unfinished Business | Excuses and Avoidance Strategies | Instances of Tension | Relaxation Techniques | Alcoholic Beverages | Cigarettes Smoked | Medications

WHAT CAUSES YOU STRESS?

Identifying Your Personal Sources of Stress

In the last section you were asked to record a recent stress-producing situation. Now you'll want to consider what you believe to be the major *sources* of your stress. List below what causes stress for you.

_____

_____

_____

_____

_____

_____

No doubt you identified sources of stress in both your personal and your professional life. Perhaps your list, like that of many other educators, included such items as:

- I have too much to do and too little time to do it.
- I have too much responsibility.
- I get feedback only when my performance is unsatisfactory.
- I have unsettled conflicts with the people with whom I work.
- I am surrounded by stress carriers: individuals who are demanding, highly anxious, indecisive, chronic complainers, and depressives.

- There is ambiguity or rigidity in my work.
- Others I work with seem unclear about the nature of my role.
- I have to interrupt my work (teaching) for new priorities (student behavior).
- I have either constant change and daily variability or deadening stability.
- Decisions or changes which affect me are made "above" me. I'm expected to carry these out though I might not believe in them, or fail to see how they relate to my school or jobs, or do not know for certain how to implement them.
- I must attend numerous meetings; many of them seem pointless.
- I feel overqualified for the work I actually do.
- I feel underqualified for the work I actually do.
- I get no personal support from the people with whom I work.
- I don't get enough interaction with adults.

I'm sure you could add others. It's not always easy to identify what triggers stressful events or to know whether they trigger a long- or short-term response. But most of us have a good sense if we'll just pay attention. The following events are listed as commonly producing stress for educators. Note how they cover the gamut from student crises and emergencies to merely annoying situations. After you read through the list, go back and check those events that are also stressful for you. Respond by using a simple, "Yes," "No," or "Sometimes."

Events Stressful for Teachers

____ The first week of the school year

____ Reorganization of classes or programs

____ Colleague assaulted at school

____ Attendance at in-service meetings

____ Notification of unsatisfactory performance

____ Overcrowded classroom

____ Preparing for a strike

____ Change in duties/work responsibilities

____ Conference with principal/supervisor

____ Involuntarily transferred

____ Managing "disruptive" children

____ Implementing new curriculum goals

____ Developing and completing daily lesson plans

____ Supervising student behavior outside the classroom

____ Threatened with personal injury

____ Dealing with community racial issues

____ Maintaining self-control when angry

____ Talking to parents about their child's problems

____ Dealing with students whose primary language is not English

____ Target of verbal abuse by student

____ Evaluating student performance or giving grades

____ Lack of availability of books and supplies

____ Dealing with staff racial issues

____ Teaching students who are "below average" in achievement level

____ Breaks during the teaching day are too few and far between

____ Taking additional course work for promotion

____ Teaching physically or mentally handicapped children (including those mainstreamed)

____ Disagreement with supervisor

____ Teacher-parent conferences

____ Seeking principal's intervention in a discipline matter

____ Maintaining student personnel and achievement records

____ Classroom evaluation

____ Denial of promotion or advancement

____ Dealing with student racial issues

____ Disagreement with another teacher

Stress Inventory

Maybe you're relieved after having read this long list, thinking, "Well, at least my situation isn't all that bad!" Or maybe you're thinking, "Yup, I have that problem too . . . and that . . . and yes, that one too!" Don't let the list intimidate or overwhelm you. Think of it as reassurance that almost anything could be a potential stressor; the trick is to determine *what is a stressor for you*. The following comprehensive inventory can help you get a better idea of what causes you stress. Note the different categories.

STRESS INVENTORY

DIRECTIONS: Place a check next to those items on the inventory that produce stress for you personally. Don't check something that you know your colleagues find upsetting but you individually do not. For example, some educators react very negatively to noise around them while they are working, while others associate it with student productivity, and still others manage to tune it out. Don't be lulled into thinking that some things "should" cause stress; the goal of this inventory is to help you note exactly what does, in fact, cause *you* stress.

I. DEALING/COPING WITH CHANGE

Yes No

___ ___ **1.** There are always new rules, regulations, and policies that require constant change and adaptation on *my* part.

___ ___ **2.** I must acquire new teaching skills, deal with new curricula, and learn new ways to teach and deal with student behavior just to keep pace with the profession and with the needs of students.

___ ___ **3.** After-school activities (monitoring dances or sporting events, going to PTA meetings) disrupt my daily routine and family life.

___ ___ **4.** It's difficult to keep abreast of the research in my area of expertise.

___ ___ **5.** Administrators have different expectations of me than they do from my peers.

II. INTERPERSONAL BEHAVIOR

___ ___ **6.** I do not interact well with colleagues, and they often disagree with me.

___ ___ **7.** My colleagues rarely get together on a social basis.

___ ___ **8.** My peers and I seldom talk about home life and personal problems.

___ ___ **9.** There is a feeling of competition rather than cooperation among educators at my school.

___ ___ **10.** I have to confront students/other teachers so that when we do interact there is an uneasy feeling.

___ ___ **11.** I worry that I am not the kind of teacher my school wants and expects.

___ ___ **12.** My teaching style does not mesh well with the needs and expectations of my administrators (or my students).

III. ROLE CLARITY

___ ___ **13.** My primary role is as disciplinarian and not as teacher.

___ ___ **14.** I feel pressure between spending time at work and with my family.

___ ___ **15.** I feel conflict between what I *must* do and what my values would have me do.

___ ___ **16.** The demands from students, fellow teachers, and administrators pull me in different directions.

Yes No

___ ___ **17.** I feel conflict between doing paperwork and spending time with students.

___ ___ **18.** I feel overtrained; my work is not sufficiently challenging.

___ ___ **19.** I do not receive clear feedback on my performance.

___ ___ **20.** I don't know whether my focus should be "curriculum centered" or "child centered."

IV. COPING WITH JOB DEMANDS

___ ___ **21.** I have too many areas of responsibility.

___ ___ **22.** Class schedules are not realistic for what I need to accomplish.

___ ___ **23.** I lack clear-cut authority to accomplish my responsibilities.

___ ___ **24.** I often spend nights and vacation time finishing my work.

___ ___ **25.** Crises and urgency are the norm where I work.

___ ___ **26.** I feel guilty for relaxing during the school day.

V. ORGANIZATIONAL STRUCTURE

___ ___ **27.** I am restricted in the use of my own ideas and creativity in improving the educational environment.

___ ___ **28.** I have little say in policymaking, even though I must implement it.

___ ___ **29.** I have little if any say in the district's goals.

___ ___ **30.** The structure of the school day is very restricting.

___ ___ **31.** There are few avenues (and incentives) for promotion.

VI. THE WORKPLACE

___ ___ **32.** My classroom is too crowded.

___ ___ **33.** I have little control over the temperature in the classroom.

___ ___ **34.** The classroom is noisy and disorderly.

___ ___ **35.** The classroom is embarrassing (furniture and carpets are tattered and soiled).

___ ___ **36.** The classroom is set up in a way that makes class discussion difficult.

___ ___ **37.** Notes or pagings from the office are frequent.

___ ___ **38.** The lighting is not adequate for the kind of paperwork I do.

___ ___ **39.** The classroom is situated along a busy hallway, making me self-conscious because everyone who walks by peers in; I am afraid to relax, and I feel I always have to look busy.

___ ___ **40.** I have no privacy.

How to Interpret Your Score

As you recall, the purpose of the inventory was to get you thinking about your own personal situation, about what causes you stress. This is not a test; there are no "right" or "wrong" answers. This assessment is a pointer, a tool to tell you where to begin to eliminate or modify the sources of stress. The knowledge of what is causing your anxiety can help you reduce it by giving "felt" stress a definition. Rather than simply saying, "Boy, am I stressed!" you can say, "I am very stressed lately; I think it has a great deal to do with the number of interruptions I am getting from the new teacher next door," or "My stress level is intolerable since the classroom setup made relaxing out of view of others impossible."

Once you know more precisely the source of your stress, once you can identify the root of the problem, you can more readily eliminate that cause. For example, the simple act of closing the door to your classroom so that you can have a quiet corner might lower your stress level significantly.

Nine Key Stressors for Educators

Of course, not all stress that educators deal with is quite so straightforward. Consider the complexities of the following nine stress-producing categories. The tensions these produce and the toll they take are in direct proportion to the teacher's ability to handle the many stresses he or she regularly confronts.

1. EXPECTATIONS.
Here stress is generated by:
- the teacher's fear that he or she will not be able to live up to his or her own expectations (or that of others)
- the habit of setting overly high or cynically low expectations

- the feeling that the personal achievements and successes of yesterday are not good enough for today
- the fear that the teacher will be found wanting because he or she is insufficiently flexible and innovative in his or her instructional methods

2. SELF-FULFILLMENT.
Here stress often arises from:
- the teacher's deep-seated feelings that his or her personal values are not given sufficient opportunity for expression within the limitations of the classroom
- the teacher's misgivings that the particular job he or she is doing in the classroom may not be fully utilizing the strengths he or she has to offer society
- the habit of thinking the "grass is greener" on the other side of the fence (in a different role, such as administration; or in a different occupation, as a business executive)
- the feeling that one is locked into an educational world and cut off from the "real world" outside

3. EGO NEEDS.
Here stress is produced by:
- the need for enhanced status and respect
- the lack of stroking from those in positions of authority
- the feeling that in spite of hard work and all one's effort, advancement is not as quick as expected
- the disappointment felt when students and colleagues do not express sufficient appreciation for a teacher's hard work
- the comparison of personal standards and effectiveness with those of someone else who seems to be more successful with less effort

- the coincidence of the other fellow getting the "lucky break"
- the shortage of money with all that it represents
- the effects of accelerating inflation which make salary increases inadequate

4. STUDENT-TEACHER RELATIONS.

In this sphere, stress is caused by:

- the realization that the classroom experience falls short in preparing students to face the demands of the outside world
- the recognition that the range of interests and abilities in a class covers so wide a spectrum that it seems impossible to meet students' individual needs
- the gnawing fear that discipline and control within the classroom and the school are deteriorating
- the anxiety that constant change in curricula and teaching methods evokes
- the apprehension that current evaluation methods are not accurately assessing the various levels of student development and progress

5. COMPETENCE.

Here stress is insidiously evoked by:

- the worry that personal finesse in communicating with students is declining
- the fear that any letdown in effort and commitment will lead to being incompetent
- the impulse to "play it safe" at the expense of feeling self-cheated
- the conviction that great teaching involves vulnerability and the willingness to undertake "high risk" lessons which may succeed but may just backfire
- the fear that declining physical powers, whether caused by increasing age or soft living, will diminish teaching competence

6. INTERNAL CONFLICTS.

In this arena, stress grows out of:

- the fear of evaluation
- the failure to do the best by one's students
- the anguish of teaching a lesson that did not succeed
- the difficulty of covering a heavy course within the scheduled time
- the increasing diversity of instructional methods and materials to be mastered
- the realization of one's personal limitations in comparison with specialists whose outstanding abilities seem so apparent
- the conviction that despite years of experience one knows so little about the process of learning
- the increase in teacher decision-making responsibilities and accountability
- the pressure to meet constantly recurring deadlines
- the pangs of guilt at different times brought on by lack of self-discipline, attacks of weariness, insufficient preparation of lessons, vacillation, and the habit of worrying molehills into mountains
- the nagging sensation that "I'm not okay," resulting from childhood experiences of inadequacy which are triggered by old tapes in the subconscious
- the suspicion that no matter how hard you try, the impact on the students will be minimal and inconsequential
- the feeling of hopelessness and helplessness in the face of spiraling local and worldwide problems

7. CONFLICTING VALUES.

In this domain, stress emerges from:

- the constant need to reorganize the how, when, where, and why of teaching priorities

- the flux and flow of conflicting educational philosophies and practices
- the frustration of trying to cope with the plurality of values and attitudes encountered in today's schools
- the suspicion that the students are not receptive enough towards those values which teachers consider basic to personal growth and social responsibility
- the perception that young people today all too often disparage tradition, knowledge, achievement, standards of excellence, and hard work
- the fear that students will graduate with an inadequate value system to cope responsibly with the moral issues of life
- the unfairness of imposing one's own value system on a "captive" audience
- the anxiety that there is little room for the teacher in a world where youth increasingly demand the freedom to "do their own thing"
- the realization that the teacher is not especially esteemed as a community leader
- the inner conflict of trying to balance one's personal beliefs with the socially-accepted norms parents expect teachers to epitomize

8. SOCIAL APPROVAL.
In this pursuit, stress comes from:

- the embarrassment of marital problems or a precarious family relationship
- the excessive time demand of teaching and the feeling that personal, family, recreational, and social priorities are shortchanged

- the inability to participate in community affairs as much as one would like to because of increasing workload and teaching responsibilities
- the changes in societal values which often make existing classroom procedures seem old-fashioned and irrelevant

9. PROFESSIONAL CONSTRAINTS.
In this labyrinth, stress is precipitated by:

- the impression of decreased authority and autonomy within the classroom
- the imposition of administrative decisions
- the frequency of interruptions from a plethora of announcements, assemblies, fire drills, extracurricular activities, field trips, student tardiness and absenteeism

You can see that the key to managing stress is awareness and self-understanding. "Know thyself" is just as important for teachers as it is for students. The more we can learn about ourselves and about what stressors are operating, the better chance we have to learn and grow and change in order to be effective in our roles.

The following stress profile for teachers is designed to help you more clearly define, on a self-scoring basis, what are the areas of stress in your life and how frequently they occur. As you read each item, evaluate the statement in terms of a period of time rather than a specific day you remember. Indicate how often the source of stress occurs by circling the number that corresponds to the frequency of occurrence. Do not read the stress profile scoring sheet until after you have completed all items.

STRESS PROFILE FOR TEACHERS

© 1991 Bettie B. Youngs, Ph.D.

PART I
Personal Analysis

Part of any profile or checkup is a background analysis. In this case, it's important to know how vulnerable you are to stress, how much resistance you have to burnout. By looking at the results of the following assessment, you can tell whether you have to be especially aware of the common stressors and take special precautions to avoid them, or whether you can handle unpleasant situations with a minimum of personal and professional disruption.

DIRECTIONS: Answer each question from **1** to **5**, with a **1** being **"Very Often"** and a **5** being **"Very Rarely."** Remember, answer as honestly as possible according to your own situation. Don't answer based on what you think you should be doing, but on what you are actually like now.

____ 1. I'm less than ten pounds overweight or underweight.

____ 2. I have at least one sit-down, relaxed meal a day; my diet is well-balanced.

____ 3. I exercise at least twenty minutes a day, three days a week, doing an aerobic exercise that increases my heartbeat.

____ 4. I get about eight hours sleep almost every night.

____ 5. I drink fewer than three cups of caffeinated drinks (coffee, tea, soft drinks) a day.

____ 6. I drink no more than two or three alcoholic drinks a week.

____ 7. I smoke very little, usually fewer than five cigarettes a day.

____ 8. I consider myself in general good health and have no specific health worries.

____ 9. I make a point of taking a few minutes a day for "down time," time to relax and unwind.

____ 10. I make a point of doing at least one activity a day just for me, something I enjoy.

____ 11. I make enough money to cover my living expenses and have no serious financial worries.

____ 12. I have a close or best friend with whom I can discuss my day on a regular basis.

____ 13. I have a wide variety of interesting friends and acquaintances with whom I do fun activities.

____ 14. I belong to a club or social organization that makes me feel accepted and wanted.

____ 15. I have good communication with my family or with the people in my household; we can talk out little annoyances before they become serious problems.

____ 16. I have a supportive family and know I can count on my relatives to help if I were ever in serious trouble.

____ 17. I am able to "blow up" and get matters off my chest, but then forget the matter and go on relatively easily.

____ 18. I am able to give and take love and affection.

____ 19. I have at least one person in my life who tells me regularly that he or she loves me.

____ 20. I am comforted by my spiritual beliefs/faith.

SCORING: Add up the numbers you assigned to each statement. Subtract 20. If your total is under 30, congratulations! You have a strong resistance to stress and are probably handling the events in your life well. If your total is between 31 and 50, you are vulnerable to stress, and should be more aware of what stressors are in your life and how well or poorly you handle them. If your score is over 51, you are extremely vulnerable to stress and need to reevaluate your lifestyle, or possibly talk with someone such as a counselor to help you get a better balance in your life.

This assessment, like the others, is a tool to help you recognize where you are at in relationship to stress. Everyone has different levels of resistance. You have seen this for physical health where some teachers catch colds the minute their first students start sneezing, while others can breeze through the worst flu epidemics with never a cough or wheeze. Similarly, the resistance of individuals to stress varies. Some people let situations "get to them," while others are not upset or affected in the least. By knowing your starting point, where you are now, you are able to know how much stress you can accept before you have to take steps to change your situation.

PART II
Negative Stressors for Teachers

If you have a low resistance to stress, you need to eliminate or reduce the negative effects of the stressors. This second part of the teacher's stress profile helps you identify those areas of your profession that cause you problems.

DIRECTIONS: Make a list of five to ten aspects of your job that you do not like, anything that causes you stress. At first, list them as they come to you. Then go back and assign priorities to each item: which causes you the most stress, which causes you the least.

Job Stressors

_____

_____

_____

_____

_____

_____

_____

_____

_____

_____

Job Stressors Ranked

1. _____

2. _____

3. _____

4. _____

5. _____

6. _____

7. _____

8. _____

9. _____

10. _____

ANALYSIS: Did you have trouble thinking of ten, or could you have gone on and on? You may find it interesting to note the Educator's Top 10 List as given in response to a study at the University of Northern Iowa. Teachers in the survey listed the following:

1. Paperwork
2. Administration
3. Non teaching duties
4. Low pay
5. Dealing with parents/community
6. Student apathy
7. Discipline
8. Other teachers
9. No time to accomplish tasks
10. Work load

Chances are you had some of these on your own list. However, you may not have listed others, not considering them stressful. Keep in mind that what is upsetting for one individual may not be for another. In fact, one teacher's stressor is another teacher's fun . . . as indicated by the next part of the profile.

PART III
Positive Stressors for Teachers

When the word "stress" is mentioned, most people immediately think of its negative aspects. But some stress can be positive. For example, juggling a career, family, social life, and self are certainly stressful, as are getting married, receiving a promotion, losing weight, and seeing your child give her first piano recital. Yet, depending on how you look at them, all of these can be desirable experiences. Some stressors can be advantageous and just plain fun. Try the following exercise:

DIRECTIONS: Following along the lines of the previous exercise, list those five to ten things about your job that you do like and do find satisfying and/or exciting. At first, just jot down the items in no particular order. Then go back and assign priorities.

_____

_____

_____

_____

_____

_____

_____

1. _____
2. _____
3. _____
4. _____
5. _____
6. _____
7. _____
8. _____
9. _____
10. _____

Perhaps the only thing more subjective than dislikes is likes. Below are the Educator's Top 10 List given by teachers in the survey discussed above. How many did you list?

1. Working with students
2. Colleagues
3. Summer vacations
4. Student progress
5. Working hours
6. Subject matter
7. Freedom to implement
8. Varied workday
9. Helping others
10. Challenge

PART IV
Managing Stress

Thus far you have diagnosed how vulnerable you are to stress and thought about both negative and positive stressors that you encounter in teaching. The last part of this stress profile deals with how well you handle those stresses.

DIRECTIONS: The following statements list common stress-coping techniques, both positive and negative. Put a "**Yes**" or "**No**" by each statement as it applies to you.

___ 1. If I know I am tense, I make the time to sit quietly and think about what's causing the tension.

___ 2. I sometimes use name-calling or blaming others for my problems when I'm under stress.

___ 3. I make certain I go out and take a walk, or get some form of exercise when it seems my day has too many pressures.

___ 4. I withdraw from others when the stresses are too great.

___ 5. I talk to others about my problems, listening to their suggestions even if I don't always act upon them.

___ 6. I sometimes overeat or take a few too many drinks in an effort to relieve stress.

___ 7. I sleep more hours when I am under stress, even taking naps during the day.

___ 8. I take prescription medication, such as tranquilizers, to help me deal with the stress.

___ 9. I use visualization, mentally picturing a peaceful scene, to take a "mind vacation" when I am under pressure.

___ 10. I work harder when things are stressful, figuring that the sooner I can get this over with, the quicker I will be able to return to my normal existence.

SCORING: For odd-numbered questions, give yourself +1 point for each "**Yes**" and -1 point for each "**No**." For even-numbered questions, give yourself -1 point for each "**Yes**" and +1 point for each "**No**." You might have a 0 score, with the good and bad coping strategies cancelling each other out. Any positive score is good. The higher the positive, the better you are at managing stress. A negative score indicates a problem area.

This stress profile took you through four steps. First, you diagnosed your own vulnerability level and saw how susceptible you are to stress. Then, you diagnosed your own stressors, positive and negative. Finally, you evaluated how well or poorly you are currently coping with stress. The goal of this profile is to make you aware of how you are doing now in order to help you prepare to deal better with stress in the future. Knowing what causes stress for you can help you develop skills and select strategies for decreasing stress in your life.

COPING WITH STRESS

By now you've come to realize that stress is virtually unavoidable. No one's life (or work) is without stress. Being stress-free does not mean living without conflict, but rather having the ability to cope with it — you achieve mastery over it.

Those who deal most effectively with stress are flexible enough to adapt to the stressors around them. They don't take themselves quite so seriously, lead a more balanced life, learn new skills to lessen the influence of the stress without feeling intimidated, and seek outside help when they recognize their need for it.

How about YOU? What are the ways you cope with your stressors? Are you more likely to:

■ Just begin your day hoping to get all the things done that you would like to?

■ Avoid exercise, especially when you're tense?

■ Let interruptions and the needs of others dominate yours?

■ Feel you don't have time to relax?

■ Skip meals when rushed?

■ Let your feelings build up and then vent your frustrations when you can no longer hold them in?

Or are you more likely to:

■ Start your day by taking 15 minutes of quiet time to get organized, then prioritize the things you must get done that day?

■ Work out several times a week, especially when you're tense?

■ Schedule "off limits" time when you need it?

■ Take time out to relax?

■ Eat breakfast each day?

■ Express your feelings clearly and in a straightforward way?

How do you "cope" or handle it when the stresses and strains of life knock at your door? Identify your personal coping behavior "style." Record it for yourself below.

When under stress, pressure, and anxiety, I:

_____

_____

_____

_____

_____

_____

Take a moment to review your response. Does your general style of coping *work for you*? In other words, is it effective, or could there be other more productive and effective ways? For example:

■ Plan downtime or idletime every day.

■ Avoid irritating and overly-competitive people prior to lunch or near the end of the school day.

■ Concentrate on one task at a time so you can enjoy your accomplishments.

■ At least three days a week make a pact with your fellow teachers at the lunch table that you won't "talk shop." Steer the discussion into personal matters or solve the problems of the world (world hunger, pollution, corruption); stay clear of more immediate problems (class size, budget cutbacks).

■ Avoid sitting with negative teachers — the stress enhancers or intensifiers.

- Spend time thinking (or talking) about what you like about your job.

- Practice mini-mind vacations where you visualize a scene that is especially comforting to you for five minutes each day.

- Interact at least once each day with someone in your school who makes you laugh.

- Think about your involvement in outside activities that provide personal satisfaction.

- Plan a free weekend every other weekend.

- Avoid situations where you have prolonged waits; for example, if going out to dinner, go before or after the usual dinner crowd.

- If you have a family, do a small but in-depth one-to-one activity with each family member during the course of each month.

- Develop a vacation attitude after work (treat your home as your vacation home).

- Live by the calendar, not by the stopwatch.

- Plan easy-going, non-structured vacations three to four days in duration.

- Get involved with a friend, your spouse, or a child in an activity that will teach you new concepts, new skills, or new processes.

- Devise a physical activities schedule, like jumping rope or riding a stationary bike, three times per week, twenty minutes each time.

DEVELOPING EFFECTIVE COPING STRATEGIES

You needn't succumb to stress nor be debilitated by it. Strategies for managing stress can be learned. By developing skills and selecting strategies for decreasing stress, you increase your psychological heartiness and resilience. This section is designed to provide you with a wide array of coping strategies. Any number of these could be effective for you, so be open-minded as you try them on to determine which ones fit you best.

Building Your Tolerance to Stress

The first coping strategy is to build your tolerance to stress. Your tolerance level is determined by your *style of reacting*. Basically, there are three styles of reacting:

1. Stimulus-based: Your reactions are determined by the importance you assign to an event. The event may be of such low priority you don't feel much stress, or you may attach so much power to it that you become stressed before the event is even played out. For example, you might get angry and defensive while driving to an appointment — before anything has happened. Perhaps you assume or anticipate that your ideas will not be met with approval, hence you get worked up before such a response is warranted.

2. Response-based: Your reactive style is the culprit. You create your own stockpile of feelings and act them out in the wrong setting or take them out on the wrong person. Has a colleague, student, spouse, or your child unfairly been the recipient of your stress response?

3. Interaction-based: You forget your priorities and goals and get baited into the emotions of the discourse, a sort of, "It's the principle of the thing that counts." You argue for something, even if you don't feel all that strongly about the outcome, or the matter is not all that value-laden and important to you.

You can strengthen your ability to tolerate stress. You can minimize your stress by assigning less power to those stress-producing events, by making them less important than they really are. You might ask yourself, "Is this really worth getting worked up over?" Take a moment to determine the importance and urgency of the action demanded so that you can respond appropriately. The goal is to learn to alter:

- Your perception of the importance and urgency of the action demanded. Ask, "Is this worth my emotions, my energy, my time?"

■ Your actual ability to cope. Ask, "Is this a lack of technique or a lack of training that causes me to react negatively to the stressor?"

■ Your cognitive appraisal. Say, "I will rehearse prior to the event and list my alternatives."

■ Your views of shared and delegated authority. Say, "I will allow myself to have faith in others' abilities and ask for help when I need it."

Remember Cristina, the educator who had one stressor after another? Let's see how she could apply these concepts to strengthen her own ability to tolerate stress.

1. The importance and urgency of the action demanded. These may be two separate concepts. Because Cristina recognized music as important to her students, she took over the music teacher's duties. However, "duties" is a very broad category and can include some activities that are important but not urgent. Cristina should determine exactly what needed to be done in terms of the music hour. If Cristina knew that she was somewhat intimidated by music and annoyed by the loud singing, she could have substituted another activity. For example, she might have looked for a record, a relaxing one that she and the children could both enjoy listening to. While learning songs for the recital is important, it could be put off for a while; it is not urgent. However, the opposite is true of the child abuse problem — it is both important and urgent.

2. Actual ability to cope. Cristina needs to decide whether she is capable of coping with the problem herself. She can almost certainly take over the music class for one time. However, she may not be able to work with the child who was abused. Cristina can delegate certain parts of that task to a counselor or nurse or someone who can give immediate attention to the problem.

3. Cognitive appraisal. Cristina can rehearse several different ways of handling a task. If she knows that her husband traditionally falls back on the taunt, "You think you're irreplaceable!" whenever he is frustrated or upset, she can practice her responses in advance. Knowing what to say and doing so calmly can prevent the situation from exploding into a full-fledged argument.

4. Views of shared and delegated responsibility. Perhaps Cristina's husband has a point; perhaps Cristina takes too much on herself, thinking that she is the hub of everything. Cristina needs to clarify her thoughts on her role. Does she do so little preparation that a substitute would not be able to follow her lesson plan and teach the class? Is she allowed one or two "personal leave" days a year, and if so, can she take that time for special occasions to be with her spouse? Can she take off a day or two without pay in order to share important travels together, should this be reasonable and necessary? Does she secretly worry that if she misses even one day, the school will see that it can in fact get along without her, thus making her feel less valuable?

The goal is to use the reaction style most appropriate for a particular situation. Suppose Bob, a fellow teacher, comes to your room during planning period, when you're busy preparing for your next class. It's obvious he wants to talk. The first question you need to answer is whether Bob wants to talk about serious matters (a discipline problem he wants advice on) or simply to socialize for a few minutes. If it's the former, you know you need to find the time for the discussion. However, if it's the latter — if Bob is looking for a few minutes of "downtime" and he just wants to chat and socialize, and you can't afford to take the time away from your task at hand — you need to make a second decision. If you feel the visit is worth the good feeling it will generate, you'll have to tolerate the time bind it may cause. If you feel negatively about the time expenditure, you must determine how much time you can honestly spare. "Bob, I've got just five minutes to enjoy your company, then it's back to getting ready for my next class."

If your style is *response-based,* you may be keyed up after Bob's visit and find it difficult to get back to the tasks at hand. For example, Bob says he's heard rumors about possible transfers. If you react to such stimuli, you may become emotionally charged, too, and have trouble concentrating. If Bob brings up matters that worry or anger you, you may have to force yourself to go beyond those feelings and get back to the matter at hand.

With a *reactive style,* you create stress for yourself by reacting long after your colleague has left. You show a reactive style when you remain calm despite the negative stimuli at school, but later at home you are tense, abrasive, or impatient with family members. In order to avoid this, you might say, "Bob, I'm all tied up right now. Can we get together later today? I'd like to talk some ideas over with you." You present a set time and show a genuine interest in seeing Bob, thus reconciling job demands with your personal needs.

Tolerance, though more passive than other forms of dealing with stress, requires that you think before you act. The following suggestions can help you build tolerance, foster acceptance, and clarify your ideas.

Steps to Building Your Stress Tolerance

1. Clarify the purpose: Whether it's a student tugging at your jacket or a principal shuffling papers and clearing her throat portentously, you can ask, "Why are you doing this? Do you want immediate action, or are you just connecting with me?" We have all had the experience of turning to a child with an exasperated sigh and a "What *now!*" only to be humbled when we find the child handing us something we mentioned we wanted or doing something else kind for us. The same is true of your peers. You may be pleasantly surprised to find that this individual across from you is not just another person wanting something more from you, but a colleague who respects your opinion and wants any input you can give him. The person may be seeking information, not action.

2. Clarify communications (and definitions): Whether dealing with a student or an adult, don't be afraid to ask, "What exactly do you mean when you say that? Could you give me a few examples that illustrate what you are saying?" Knowing and translating what the other person *means* can save you a lot of mistakes and stress.

3. Clarifying the sources of ideas: Students place a great deal of confidence in "they," as in, "They say that if we do well on this test, we won't have to take the final next week." Who are "they?" Ask the students to specify where they get their information. Find out whether their statements are personal opinions or facts that are supported by data. Knowing that a statement is supportable makes you more comfortable in using it later, less worried that it may rebound against you somewhere down the line.

4. Clarify the length of an idea: Children change their points of view with breathtaking speed. Sometimes our colleagues seem to be doing the same. Ask questions like, "Have you always felt like that, or has something happened recently to change your mind? Do you think you will continue to feel this way, or are you open to change?" Knowing how firm an opinion is can indicate how much time and effort you will need to allot to working with a student or colleague. If he is dogmatic and utterly convinced he is right, you will have to put in more hours talking to him and showing him your side than you would with a more flexible person.

5. Point out inconsistencies: Ask yourself, "Is this idea or concept inconsistent with what others are doing or saying?" Knowing whether there are in fact real differences, or whether the differences are only a matter of misinterpretation, can help you relax and not see difficulties where none exist.

6. Question usefulness: Ask, "Will this be beneficial for us? Can we make the idea work for our class, our school?" Take a few minutes to think about the feasibility of the plan rather than become stressed later over having wasted time on something that really stood little chance of success in the first place.

7. Considering alternatives: Ask, "What other choices might we make?" Recognizing that you have options can relieve some of the pressure on you. It's important to know that you have more than one course of action available.

8. Summarize: Ask, "Can we rephrase in just a few words the important ideas or concepts here?" If you cannot do so, you do not yet fully understand them. If you don't have a complete understanding, you'll have defeated the purpose of asking questions in the first place and are well on your way to creating, not eliminating, stress.

EMOTIONAL MANAGEMENT AS A TOOL

When others attack your ideas, goals, and dreams, when you feel excluded, when your pride and esteem are in jeopardy, and/or when financial or political security appear uncertain, stress can cause you to be defensive and fearful. You can learn to counteract some of your internal defense mechanisms. The first step is to look at how you perceive events.

A common cause of stress is something known as the *tyranny of the shoulds*. When you feel that you "should" do something, but you cannot or simply don't want to, stress builds. Take, for example, the idea of time management. Of course, you recognize the importance of using time efficiently, the desirability of effective time management. You may have the best intentions in the world of getting a lot done

as you stride into your classroom in the morning. But within a few minutes all those good resolutions may be mere memories. Maybe there's an unsettled dispute between two students that is carrying over into the classroom, distracting everyone and taking up precious time that should be used for course instruction. A student doesn't understand that you spent hours getting your lesson plan done well, that you took all last night blocking out your time modules, and that you will need all the class hour to deliver the lesson.

Good things can disrupt your calendar as well: Maybe the class becomes so wonderfully excited about your lecture that they want to continue the discussion long after the allotted time has passed. If you try to cover every possible contingency, you'll be so preoccupied with the problem of time that you'll not be giving students the best of yourself. You will lose your peace of mind and will feel continually insecure . . . in a word, stressed.

Cognitive Restructuring

Sometimes we *feel, act,* and then *think,* when we would be well served to *think, feel,* and then *act. Thoughts determine behaviors.* You've no doubt experienced this principle in operation. While driving, you begin to think about an unpleasant confrontation you had with someone a day, week, or month earlier. Soon you're driving faster and clenching the wheel tightly. Recalling the details of the situation has made you upset all over again, yet it's just you in the car — you're alone! Recalling the incident produced the same emotions as if it had just happened.

Perhaps you have heard someone say, "I can't help what I do, it just happens." This assumes that thoughts and feelings occur independently and are not under our control. However, the opposite is true. Rarely does a feeling "just happen." There's a direct connection between thoughts, feelings, and behaviors. Let's look at this in operation.

Dr. Henderson reprimands you for letting a student out of class without a restroom pass. He says, "I know you're a Mentor teacher, Julie, but you have to follow the rules like everyone else." Julie begins to process this message. Here are two possible scenarios of her thinking.

> **Julie's Thoughts:** "Dr. Henderson is mad at me. He knows how much I sacrifice for these kids. If he had any appreciation for my work and dedication, he would let me slide on minor infractions."
>
> **Julie's Feelings:** Upset, angry, defensive.
>
> **Julie's Behavior:** She avoids going to the teachers' lounge for lunch, because she knows he brings his lunch there to visit with the teachers.

Here Julie assumes that it's Dr. Henderson who made her upset and angry, and that she, therefore, has a right to be defensive. After all he did reprimand her. In this case, what Julie is thinking is irrational and it affects her behavior in a negative way. A different and more positive scenario on Julie's part might be as follows.

> **Julie's Thoughts:** "I wish I hadn't let Tommy out without a pass. I know how hard our staff has been working to monitor and reduce the numbers of students wandering around in the halls without a pass. I put Tommy at risk for being sent to the principal's office. I know the rules, and it doesn't feel good to be reminded by someone whose support I want."
>
> **Julie's Feelings:** Rational, feeling responsible.

> **Julie's Behavior:** "I'm sorry, Dr. Henderson. I know I'm supposed to give the kids a pass. I guess I made a bad judgment call with Tommy for the sake of convenience."

The connection between thinking and behavior is this: it's not so much the event that determines behavior as how you think about it.

Thought-Stopping

Once you're aware of how inner thoughts work for or against you, you'll want to be able to change the negative thoughts to positive ones. This procedure is called thought-stopping. What this means is that you visualize a stop sign whenever you start telling yourself limiting statements. This stop sign acts as a signal to stop thinking dysfunctional thoughts. The last phase of thought-stopping involves thought-substitution. Here you would generate as many positive thoughts as possible:

> "Just because Dr. Henderson called me on not giving Tommy a pass doesn't mean he doesn't like me."
>
> "Just because Dr. Henderson called me on not giving Tommy a pass does not mean he doesn't consider me a good teacher," and so on.

Rescripting Messages

Another way you can turn negative thoughts into positive ones is by reshaping the message.

> **Example:** I don't like my fourth period class.
>
> **Rewrite:** I enjoy all my classes except fourth period. I know how difficult it must be for students to come back from lunch to a lecture format, especially when I have so many reluctant learners who need special assistance with the learning skills and who lack motivation in the first place.

Just like a student who thinks he's not a good student will find school difficult (and this will contribute to his not liking school), how you view the situation (in this case fourth period) determines how you will deal with it as well.

Changing, rewriting, or rescripting the way you think is a vital skill in reducing and managing stress because when we send mostly positive messages to ourselves, we are more likely to have the courage to straighten things out when they get tough. When we face and overcome challenges, we start an invigorating and contagious success cycle that contributes to our performance and productivity, to our self-esteem, and to an empowering presence in our relationships with students and colleagues.

Jordan is a new teacher at Central Middle School. Today he has to meet with Carole, the head of the PTA. Carole has had three children go through this school, and her fourth child is in his class. Carole feels that she should inform him on *how things are done*. She takes up hours of Jordan's time, telling him about how things have always been done in the past and the ideas she has for new projects that would benefit her child. She is also not above gossiping about other teachers and parents. When Jordan walks into his class in the morning and turns the page of his organizer, he sees Carole's name. He has an appointment with her after school. He gives a groan that makes a passing teacher stick his head in and ask whether he is feeling all right. "It's okay, Cliff, it's just that Carole Schultz again. I know I should look on the good side and try to be grateful that she is so involved and willing to share her knowledge with me, but I can't help thinking of her as a time-waster."

Within the next hour, Jordan has a headache and a toothache (from gritting his teeth in frustration) and a stiff neck. By the time Carole enters Jordan's room, Jordan is ready to lay the blame for all his stress on the smiling PTA president. But who really has caused the problems? Did Carole give Jordan the sore jaw, the headache,

the stiff neck? No, of course not. Jordan controls his own body and emotions. What can he do to prevent such problems? As an example, he can change his outlook on the scheduled appointment with Carole.

Jordan already knows of his problem. He admits that he "should" feel differently. So what's stopping him? Jordan has control over his own emotions. It may not be easy to do, but it is possible for him to decide to listen patiently. By deciding ahead of time that he's going to listen with the goal of learning something rather than suffer with the goal of surviving, Jordan can make the experience much less stressful. By restructuring his feelings, he can change his own inner emotions. The point is this: The way you think influences your behavior and thus your responses to stressful situations. What you say to yourself before, during, and after an incident greatly influences your feelings and behaviors. Recall a recent stressful event and see whether you can trace this process for yourself.

Describe a recent stressful *event*:

_____

_____

_____

_____

_____

_____

What were you *thinking?*

_____

_____

_____

_____

_____

_____

What did you do as a result of your thinking (*behavior*)?

_____

_____

_____

_____

_____

_____

_____

Note how your behavior was influenced by your thinking process and not necessarily by the event itself. To help you see the importance of this idea, let's do one possible "rewrite" of Jordan's stressful event. Instead of thinking, "This woman drives me nuts; the afternoon is going to be wasted," he could have thought, "I have an opportunity to hear the 'inside story' from a parent who cares enough to be involved. I am grateful that we have parents like this. And you know, we must have done something right with her other children if she takes time out of her busy day to come to talk to me. Obviously, she respects me enough to want to keep me informed."

Jordan has the right idea with this "rewrite," which will affect his thinking in a positive way, thus changing his actions and making him more effective in this encounter. He might actually look forward to speaking with Carole. And by congratulating himself on doing a good enough job to make her want to keep him informed, he treats her entire visit as a compliment to him rather than as a problem.

Now you try it. Using the same event you wrote down when you described a recent stressful event, "rewrite" another path you could have chosen in your thinking. How would this have resulted in different behavior?

The *event:*

_____

_____

_____

_____

_____

Your revised *thinking:*

_____

_____

_____

_____

_____

_____

Resulting *behavior:*

_____

_____

_____

_____

_____

PROTECTING YOUR SELF-ESTEEM

We understand the importance of a positive sense of self for our students, and therefore constantly work to build self-esteem in children, but it's important that we nurture ours as well. We too need a base of confidence, positive energy, inspiration, courage, drive, and strength of character in order to sustain high levels of top-notch competence. The possession of high self-esteem is not a prerequisite to being effective in our work, but when low, it erodes our ability to manage daily stress and pressures.

High self-esteem is criteria number one for the educator. Just as a student with a positive sense of self is better able to take on the challenge and rigors associated with learning — and therefore is more likely to find school purposeful and rewarding — the educator with a positive sense of self is better able to take on the extraordinary challenges associated with teaching and working with youth — and in doing so, bring confidence, know-how, high energy, a "can do" competence, and performance to the role — over and over again each day, even in the face of daily obstacles. As a result, the educator is more likely to find teaching purposeful and rewarding.

Self-esteem is central not only to what each of us will achieve in the course of our lifetime, but it is at the heart of what we make of our lives — the loyalty we bring to developing ourselves and to caring for others. Perhaps nothing affects health and energy, peace of mind, the goals we set and achieve, our inner happiness, the quality of our relationships, our competence, performance and productivity, quite so much as the health of our self-esteem.

Perhaps you've heard the term *self-esteem* defined as "how much you like yourself." Self-esteem is much more than that. *Self-esteem* is a composite picture of perceived self-value. For example, you might think a particular student has everything going for him, but inside *he* may not see himself in that way. No doubt you've looked at students who are unsure of themselves and thought, "I wonder if Jane has any idea how capable she is!" "If only Tom knew how bright he is!" In other words, your view and the student's view differ. Your perception of your worth is the essence of self-esteem. There are six powerful ingredients of self-esteem:

The Six Ingredients of Self-Esteem

1. A Sense of Physical Safety: Feeling physically safe means that you aren't fearful of being harmed or hurt. You feel safe — in your school, home, and neighborhood. You care for your body, knowing that you must protect yourself from anything that could put your health in jeopardy (such as danger, drugs and alcohol or other substances, and so on).

2. A Sense of Emotional Security: When you know you won't be put down or made to feel less worthy, and when you feel you can confront and deal with your fears, you feel emotionally secure. You feel secure that others won't beat you up emotionally with sarcasm or hurtful words (and that includes things you say to yourself!). You are respectful, considerate, and friendly — to yourself and others. You believe that as a human being you have worth, and you feel deserving of other people's care.

3. A Sense of Identity: Knowing yourself, *self-knowledge*, allows you to develop a realistic and healthy sense of individuality. You are friends with the face in the mirror. You've taken the time to get to know and understand yourself. In turn, knowing and accepting yourself allows you to care about others. You treat yourself with respect, and want them to respect you in return.

4. A Sense of Belonging: When you feel accepted, liked, appreciated and respected by others, you show respect and acceptance in return. You work for harmony in those relationships. While you stand up for yourself, you don't ignore the opinions of others — you are willing to hear them out. But you don't depend on their views to make your decisions. You cannot be easily swayed into making choices that are out of line with what you know to be right for you. You strive for interdependence.

5. A Sense of Competence: Feeling capable gives you the motivation to achieve. When you feel sure of yourself and your abilities, you feel in charge of your life. You feel capable of coping with the challenges in your life. You're willing to try new things, to develop and expand your abilities, to persevere rather than give up when a situation becomes difficult.

You're aware of your strengths, and while you also know of those areas where you are less capable, you lead with your strengths.

6. A Sense of Purpose: You set and achieve goals that are important to you. You know your values and are living your life according to those values. Your values are reflected in your behaviors, and your actions are a reflection of your values. Life has meaning and direction.

You don't just wake up one day with a bad self-esteem or a good self-esteem, or with a high self-esteem or a low self-esteem. It's developed over time. A healthy self-esteem is a result of actively participating in your life in a meaningful way. For example, you promise to be your own best friend, to always stick by yourself in good times and bad. You take responsibility for your choices, actions, and behaviors. You work towards those goals that are important to you. You actively work to change those things that aren't working well for you. You live your life according to a plan that you yourself have devised and approved.

There are many benefits of having a high self-esteem. They include:

■ The higher your self esteem, the better able you are to cope with the ups and downs of your life.

■ The higher your self-esteem, the more likely you will think about what you want out of life, the more ambitious you will be in going after it, and the more likely you will achieve it.

■ The higher your self-esteem, the better able you will be to attract others who enjoy their lives and are working to their potential. Individuals with low self-esteem tend to seek low self-esteem friends who also think poorly of themselves.

■ The higher your self-esteem, the more likely you will treat others with respect and fairness, since self-respect is the basis of respect for others.

■ The higher your self-esteem, the more you will confront obstacles and fears rather than avoid them. Low esteem individuals see problems as grounds for quitting, and often say to themselves, "I give up."

■ The higher your self-esteem, the better able you will be in finding ways to get along well with others. You strive to be useful, helpful, and responsive.

■ The higher your self-esteem, the more compassion you will show for yourself and for others. Compassion exposes self-worth: When you have discovered the treasured value of your personhood, you care about the value of others too.

■ The higher your self-esteem, the more secure, decisive, friendly, trusting, cheerful, optimistic, and purposeful you are. We call this being *empowered*.

■ The higher your self-esteem, the more able you are to recognize your own worth and achievements without a constant need for approval from others.

■ The higher your self-esteem, the more responsibility you take for your own actions.

■ The higher your self-esteem, the more willing you are to hang in there, even when the going gets tough. Because you persist, the greater are your chances for experiencing success. Since you have experienced previous successes, you are less likely to be devastated by periodic setbacks.

■ The higher your self-esteem, the better able you are to cope with problems because you feel you have the ability to resolve them.

Self-esteem, then, is a consequence. It's your total "score" (or *value*). This score becomes *your* price tag, so to speak. Self-esteem is the way *you* see yourself: It is very personal. The overall health of your self-esteem can render you psychologically hardy or vulnerable, capable or incapable, vivacious, or despondent. We all want and need to matter, to feel important (most especially to ourselves). This is true for children as it is for adults. Each one of us needs to know that we are giving our time — the substance of our life — to something very special. That's why teaching can be very emotionally rewarding and fulfilling when we feel that we are making a difference, or desperately trying, unrewarding and stressful when we feel we aren't.

By strengthening our self-esteem, we lessen the power of stressful events. Books like *Enhancing The Educator's Self-Esteem: It's Your Criteria #1* can be a real help in building the educator's self-esteem. The resource section at the end of this book lists additional resources.

PROFESSIONAL SUPPORT SYSTEMS

Having a base of peer support can be a cushion in reducing stress. Getting together with colleagues who will listen and share feelings and thoughts (and strategies that work in a variety of situations) can be as therapeutic as it is networking. A candid exchange in a safe environment can lower the collective stress level. I serve as a consultant in a school district where teachers in one school get together for dinner one Tuesday a month with the staff in another school. The function serves as a way to exchange ideas and discuss how teachers cope with professional and personal roles, to share what works, when, and why. Such a support system reduces feelings of alienation, empowers and refuels the self-esteem of each of its members, and provides comradery — the insulation that can prevent burnout.

Not all support groups look alike. The important thing is that you feel connected. Who are the members of your professional support system? Take a moment and identify them:

Name: _____
What this person does to demonstrate support:

_____

_____

_____

_____

_____

Name: _____
What this person does to demonstrate support:

_____

_____

_____

_____

Name: _____
What this person does to demonstrate support:

_____

_____

_____

SOCIAL/PERSONAL SUPPORT SYSTEMS

In addition to your professional support group, there are family and friends who can provide protection during stressful times. With them you can share your thoughts, feelings, and opinions. Raising a family and putting in long hours at our work can make us feel like we rarely spend time with friends, or that we have fewer than we actually do. Take the time now to list who in your personal life provides support, advice, and comfort during stressful times:

Name: _____

What this person does to demonstrate support:

_____

_____

_____

_____

Name: _____

What this person does to demonstrate support:

_____

_____

_____

_____

Name: _____

What this person does to demonstrate support:

_____

_____

_____

_____

Individuals who have developed close friendships, strong family ties, and warm relationships with friends and peers, deal more effectively with stressful events than those who are socially isolated. Do you need to expand your network? There are many ways in which you can. For example, by joining a social organization, sports club, or church group, you can broaden your range of interests and activities. By demonstrating your interest in others, in their ideas and activities and feelings, you provide the basis for mutually fortifying relationships.

Other people are an essential part of our lives. They provide objectivity, reassurance, fun and warmth, and perspectives. There are

glass balls and rubber balls in life. The goal is to know which is which. *Family, health, and friends are the glass balls. You must NEVER drop the glass balls.* Respect and care for these relationships: when they are not working they produce a good share of the pain and stress we feel. When intact, they provide a potent source of good feelings that are an important source of our sound emotional health.

EFFECTIVE COMMUNICATION SKILLS

Communicating effectively can both prevent and defuse stress. When you communicate openly, honestly, and caringly, you create a climate for one of the most basic human needs — expression. You're telling the other person that he or she is valuable, worth your time and attention.

The responsibility for communicating effectively rests with you. In the long run, whether talking or listening, you must assume a good share of the responsibility for the results you get. Have you ever heard someone say (or said it yourself!), "*You* made me so mad?" instead of saying, "*I've* become upset with . . .?" There are a number of skills necessary in communicating effectively. Four of the essential ones are:

■ Gaining Understanding

■ Active Listening

■ Giving and Receiving Feedback

■ Problem Solving

Seeking to Understand

Communicating involves or entails a willingness to *understand* the other person. The first rule in communicating effectively is to seek first *to understand*, and then to be understood. Stephen Covey, author of *The 7 Habits of Highly Effective People*, gives a humorous analogy to this end:

Suppose that you think you need glasses. You go to the optometrist for help. He briefly listens to your complaint and then takes off his glasses and hands them to you.

"I'm sure you need glasses," he says. "Here, I've worn this pair for a few years now, and they've really helped me. I think you'll find them helpful, too. Take this pair; I have an extra pair at home."

You try them on. "But I can't even see out of them," you say.

"Well, what's wrong?" he asks. "They work great for me. Try harder. You'll get used to them," he says.

"I am trying, but everything looks like a blur."

"Well, think positively."

"Okay, I positively can't see a thing!"

"Boy, are you ungrateful," he says, a little put off that he's given you his own pair, and you're rejecting them.

The foolishness here is apparent. We sometimes have the tendency to rush in and try to fix things by our standards, but fail to really deeply understand the problem first. The other person wants to know that you understand *him*, his perspective, at this moment.

It takes time and effort to understand others, and sometimes we feel we don't have all day to sit and listen. But in fact it takes far more time to deal with misunderstandings and hard feelings. When we take the time to stay with the listening process until the other person feels that we have understood, we have communicated many things: we want to understand; we care; we respect the other person's feelings; we value his or her friendship; in short, we value the relationship. Our children and marriage partners and colleagues spend a great deal of time, effort, and energy fighting for acceptance from us, for being respected, and for a sense of their own worth. *When we grant them this by sincerely seeking to understand, we find that almost all of their struggles will cease*. There are three ground rules for doing this:

■ **Show Empathy.** We can influence or persuade others only to the degree they feel we *understand* and appreciate them and are seeking their best interests as well as our own. While someone is talking, keep quiet and just listen — without waiting for your turn to talk. Sometimes we need to rise above always seeing through our own frame of reference. Autobiographical responses seldom have meaning when the other person is angry, frustrated, or stressed out. When you're concerned only about giving *your* side of the story, the listener realizes you've stopped understanding *his* moment — his need to get you to see his point of view. Take the time to listen.

■ **Listen Emphatically.** Listening emphatically means that you are listening so the other person will talk, and talking so he will listen. You are listening with the eyes and heart to feelings and not just with the ears to words. This doesn't mean that you feel as he or she feels (that's sympathy), but you are wanting to *see* the world as the other person sees it. The attitude of "I want to understand you" is enormously attractive because it keeps you open, and the other person feels that you can be influenced. What he or she says has a chance of being heard and considered. The key to your having influence with the other person is his perceiving that he has influence with you.

■ **Be Authentic.** After seeking to understand the other person's point of view, you then need to express how you see and feel about what they've said. Know what you're feeling and express it simply: "I feel . . ." "In my opinion . . ." "As I see it . . ." Giving *you* messages, "Why are *you* so stubborn," "You're so insensitive," only stirs up defenses and stops the communication process. Personalize the message. *Own* your words. At this point, avoid jumping in with how you would have handled or resolved the issue at hand.

The following three-step process will help you practice this powerful way of influencing:

■ **Mimic the content of the communication.** Simply repeat exactly what is said. If the person says, "Nobody around here ever cares what I have to say!" you say, "No one around here ever cares what you have to say?" Be patient and calm and look at the other person as you say this. The key is to parrot the phrasing, no matter how dramatic or absurd, to let the person know you have heard what he said. Perhaps in your repetition he will finally hear himself as well.

■ **Reflect feeling.** When we reflect feeling, we listen with our eyes to capture the nature and the intensity of the emotion behind the communication. In fact, the other person may be saying a great deal more with his face or with the tone of his voice than the words alone convey. For instance, the person might say, "I told Mrs. Helenak that if she ever needed anything to just call on me, but then when the assembly was scheduled, she asked me to keep her three most incorrigible students because they hadn't earned a right to go. I might as well forget about getting my work done." Reflecting the feeling, you might say, "You're pretty upset and feel completely misunderstood."

■ **Combine rephrasing content and reflecting feelings.** Here you're not agreeing or disagreeing, only attempting to reflect your understanding of what the person says and feels. Sometimes it's obvious to both parties that understanding has taken place. There is simply no need to reflect or rephrase anything. Words would be out of place, perhaps even condescending or insulting. When you hear the heated discussion of a colleague's run-in with a student, for example, your face might show a caring expression. Caring *is* the message.

Active Listening

Active listening means that you are listening attentively not only to the content of *what* is being said but to *how* it's being said. It means that you are attending fully to the words someone is speaking and, in a nonjudgmental manner, observing the feelings he or she is expressing. When the speaker has completed sharing his thoughts, you feed back your perception of the meaning of what has been said. This allows you to check his or her intention and your understanding of it. In the following example Roberta is an active listener.

Gerald walks into the lounge where his colleague Roberta is talking on the phone to a parent. Gerald mutters, "I can never get any work done around here!"

"You sound annoyed," says Roberta, when she has finished her conversation. "Are you just frustrated, or are you upset at me?"

Replies Gerald, "I'm frustrated because I have a dozen or more calls that have to be made today, and I'm not in the mood. I'm not angry at you. If you're finished with the phone, I guess I might as well begin."

Active listening defuses stress because one person acknowledges what another person is feeling. In this case Roberta's listening and questioning made clear that Gerald was indeed frustrated and upset. Secondly, her listening clarified the direction of the anger. Was it a personal, vindictive anger? Or was her colleague upset about an event, not with Roberta? Gerald was actually frustrated with the task of making a number of calls, none of which he had wanted to place.

Thirdly, active listening allows you to decide if you want to participate in someone else's frustration. Roberta has an opportunity to show empathy toward her colleague (she might have removed herself from the situation without working toward a resolve) and thus alleviate some of Gerald's frustrations. As an example, Roberta can suggest that Gerald use the phone now since her own calls are not quite as urgent. These colleagues can take the opportunity to share empathy; they can elect to value and thus preserve their relationship.

The crucial dimension in listening is understanding, which builds another's trust and confidence. When you listen, you make it clear that you care about the other person's interests, concerns, needs, hopes, fears, doubts, and joys. Listening is really a matter of acceptance: It's accepting another person's ideas and feelings, and being comfortable with the fact that their viewpoint might be different from yours. Understand that from the other person's point of view, he or she *is right*. Instead of saying, "I don't care what you think," say, "This is the way I see it." If you say in a cheerful tone, "Good, you see it differently. I would like to understand how you see it," this conveys, "I see it differently," rather than, "I'm right and you're wrong." Such an attitude admits: "Like mine, your views and feelings are legitimate and respectable." "You matter to me; I want to understand you." "I do not question how important this is to you, or your sincerity." "I care about our relationship and want to resolve this difference in perception." "Please help me to see it from your point of view." "I'm open to influence and prepared to change if necessary." Your communicating behavior reflects, "I listen to understand." "I speak to be understood." "I enter into communication from a point of agreement and move slowly into areas of disagreement."

Communication Breakdown Is a Credibility Problem

There are a number of deadly barriers that most certainly will stop communication between you and the other person. Avoid them; they'll do nothing but turn the other person off from wanting to communicate with you.

■ **Don't criticize.** The greatest single barrier to open, honest communication is the tendency to criticize.

■ **Don't hurry it.** "C'mon, C'mon. I don't have all day." Don't demand that the person disclose his heart and mind at breakneck speed. Abraham Maslow, the famous psychologist from Brandeis University, said, "He that is good with a hammer tends to think everything is a nail." This is the wrong approach for understanding someone's mind and heart.

■ **Don't judge.** Listen without judging. You want the other person to feel that she can come to you with a triumph to be shared or a problem to be discussed. You want to foster an environment of trust and enjoyment of each other's company. To achieve this atmosphere it's important that you not be judgmental. No one wants to participate in a conversation where one person is sitting on high, handing down a judgment.

Giving and Receiving Feedback

Another important element of effective communication is giving and receiving *feedback* — appropriately. As an educator, one of your primary on-going tasks is evaluating students daily via grades. Parents call up or meet with you to discuss their children's progress. You may have to do peer review. If you are fortunate, you have a bright and caring administrator who actively solicits your opinion on her policies and activities. She often asks you questions such as, "How's your year going?" "How are you doing?" "How am I doing?" "How can I assist you in meeting the needs of your students?"

When you speak of changing the "system," it's not difficult to be objective and professional. But what happens when you speak of changing the individuals within the system: teachers, students, yourself? Giving and receiving feedback can produce insecurities for all involved. Learning to give feedback constructively *can* be done. The following guidelines can get you started.

1. *Describe the situation clearly.* Identify precisely the behavior that you would like changed. Don't take refuge in generalities like, "Well, we seem to have a problem with tardiness." Instead, point out the problem clearly. "Jim, this is the third time this month you have arrived late. Even though the first few minutes are announcements, not class, you *must* be here on time."

2. *Express your own feelings.* Two points to remember when expressing your feelings will keep the exchange from becoming an emotional battle. First, take responsibility for your emotions. Second, discuss how you are feeling about the event without allowing the feedback process to act as an emotional release. "Jim, I worry that you are setting a bad example for the other students by being late so often. I am also concerned that you are not taking your studies and the school rules very seriously."

3. *Specify the changes that you would like to see occur.* Simply stating what you do not like does not guarantee that the other person (especially a child) will know what you want. It is appropriate to ask for a change in the other person's behavior. The more specific you are, the more likely it is that you will be understood. "Therefore, Jim, I would like to ask that you be here on time from now on. Your first period begins at 8:00; I'd like to see you here by 7:59."

4. *State what you perceive to be the possible consequences of a change in the other person's behavior.* Tell the other person what the result will be if your request is granted. "Seeing you here on time will change my mind about sending a note home to your parents. I have considered writing or calling them; your changing your ways right now will prevent my having to do so."

Wouldn't it be great if we were able to criticize others yet never receive any criticism ourselves? As educators know all too well, criticism goes with the territory, and not all of it feels *constructive*! We often feel as though there is a sign over our door saying, "Complaint Department." Parents, public, media, all feel eligible to speak their minds as to how we are doing. The following guidelines can help you *receive* as well as give negative feedback.

1. *Determine whether the source is reliable.* Decide how much credence to put in the criticism before you accept the feedback.

2. *Separate the emotions of the speaker from the content of the feedback.* Overlook the attitude and work on the content so that you can address the problem and resolve it.

3. *Analyze your own emotions.* Before you let your emotions overwhelm you, determine their cause.

4. *Listen before you react.* It may take an act of heroic proportions to hear out the speaker before jumping to your own defense, but try. What he or she has to say may give you clues to how you can best resolve it expediently.

5. *Put yourself in the other person's position.* It probably took a lot of nerve to approach you in the first place. Why are they telling you this? Do they really mean to be helpful? Would you offer the same back?

6. *Clarify the feedback.* Paraphrase the other person's comments, making certain you understand them. This is essential in the case of students, who might not have the vocabulary to say precisely what they mean. Ask the other person to tell you *exactly* what changes he wants. Say, "What would you like me to do about this?"

Solving Problems, Generating Alternatives, and Evaluating Consequences

When you take responsibility, when you take charge over your own actions, you feel capable. *You* are able to make decisions and choose what the outcome will be. Having a problem and not knowing how to remedy it, on the other hand, can be as debilitating as it is frustrating. Finding a solution and getting out of a dilemma is made even more difficult when you aren't sure what the problem is, only that one exists.

Effective problem solving is a four-step process that involves identifying the real problem, searching for sound solutions and recognizing the consequences, trying them out, then evaluating the outcome.

This process begins by asking four simple questions:

1. What is the problem?
2. How can I solve it? What are the consequences?
3. What is my plan?
4. How did I do?

1. What Is the Problem? Mrs. Helenak is taking her class to an assembly in the auditorium and leaving me with the three students who are known to be "behavior problems." Because I had once told her to "call on me if you need me," Mrs. Helenak has asked me to keep these students in my room during my prep period, the time I had set aside to write up a student exam. Besides, I don't want to baby-sit these three rowdy students.

2. How Can You Solve It? What Are the Consequences? Generate as many alternatives to the problem as you can and then assess the potential impact of each option. Examine the

likely outcome of proposed actions by asking questions such as, "If I do that, what will happen?" followed by, "And then what would happen?" A few examples are given to get you started.

Action: I could just smile and say I'll do it.
Consequence: I am counting on writing the exam for my class tomorrow so I don't have to take it home. I probably won't get that exam prepared if I have those three boys in my room.

Action: I could tell her, "No way! I'm not getting stuck with those three musketeers!"
Consequence: She'll feel that I'm not a trustworthy colleague.

Continue generating all the possible actions you can take and the consequences, as you see them.

Action:
Consequence:

Action:
Consequence:

3. What Is the Plan? In other words, what are you going to *do specifically*? When will you do it? What *specifically* will you *say*?

The plan is:
I am going to:
I will do this (when):

4. How Did You Do? What exactly happened as a result of following through on your plan?

What happened was:

Don't forget to teach problem-solving skills to your students. Their ability to effectively solve some of their own problems can significantly reduce stress for you. Here's an example of this process for the elementary age student:

1. What Is the Problem?

Danny called me "stupid" and it made me mad!

2. How Can I Solve It?

Action: I could call him stupid back.
Consequence: He will stay angry.

Action: I could punch him.
Consequence: He might hit me back.

Action: I could tell him how angry it makes me.
Consequence: He would understand my feelings.

Action: I could ignore it.
Consequence: He might continue to call me names.

3. What Is My Plan? Ask the students: "When will you do this?"

Action: I'm going to tell him to stop name-calling. I'll tell him on the bus tomorrow morning.

4. How Did I Do?

My plan worked great. I said it politely. I didn't get in a fight. Danny said he was sorry.

PRIORITIZING AND TIME MANAGEMENT

You are grading student essays. As you're reading them, the office secretary calls you on the intercom about an overdue form. You get out that file to work on it, but in doing so your eye catches the "urgent" pile. The top note is from the teacher with whom you are a co-advisor for the speech team. He needs to see you about an upcoming meeting. You heave a sigh, put the file away, and head down the hall. On the way you see a student who you believe is skipping class. You confront the student and then head off to his second period instructor to see whether he really is skipping or is in fact excused from class. As you pass the lounge, you see Stan Thompson there and stop to chat for a moment, but it turns into more like a half an hour. On your way back to your classroom you pass the office and decide to stop in and call Cara Daye's mother. Once inside the office, you realize the phone number is in your room.

Does this sound like you on a typical day, pulled in a dozen directions at once, starting many tasks but finishing few? If you have a tendency to be easily distracted, to shotgun your efforts, to react to every immediate situation, you'll wind up with a great deal of stress because you will accomplish very little.

What can you do? The obvious answer is to eliminate the causes. But it's not going to be possible to change all the demands on your time. There may always be more tasks to do than you have time for. Is your situation hopeless? Are you doomed like Sisyphus always to push a rock up a hill only to see it fall back down again?

Not necessarily, though it can seem like it. Begin by making a Must Do List. List the three most important jobs that you generally face every day. Then tackle them one at a time. The regularity of these tasks does reduce stress. Don't leave any of these three Must Do items half-done. Educators who decide on the priority of the tasks at hand stick with it and feel a great sense of satisfaction when they finish.

Once you work your way through the Must Do List, refer to the second tier of tasks. Once again, prioritize these tasks, listing what must be done in order of their importance. By arranging the tasks in this way, you feel as if you're exceeding the demands on yourself, that you're mastering them rather than them beating you. Here's a sample of how this might work:

Must Do List

1. Meet with counselors to discuss outside help in test preparation program. Review consultants' proposals before meeting. Check funds in budget for program.

2. Write article for district paper summarizing our recent successful senior-freshman "big brother/sister" program. Interview two or more sets of senior-freshman "couples" to get quotes.

3. Meet with librarian to discuss her complaints of my class's actions in the media center. Prepare a list of compromise solutions before meeting.

Secondary Tasks

1. Meet with principal to discuss transportation for field trips. Find figures of costs for different kinds of buses.

2. Begin preparation for semester final exams.

3. Draft letter for parents on students' accomplishments this year.

When you are compiling this list, scrutinize each task carefully. Ask yourself three basic questions:

1. *Can this task be delegated?* Is this particular task one that requires your personal touch or can it be done by someone else (a classroom assistant, a responsible and mature student) maybe with just a review or a little help from you?

2. *What would happen if this task were not done today?* If the result would be negative or would cause you a great deal of stress (maybe the task could be put off to another day, but doing so would just make you worry about it one day longer), then do it today.

3. *Is this task-imposed on me by the system, or is it self-imposed?* There are some things you just *have* to do as a part of your job, and there are other tasks that you have convinced yourself you have to do. For example, the system may require that you observe another teacher at least twice a semester. You may have set yourself the task of writing a letter regarding each observation. Is that letter essential? Could you maybe have a five-minute conversation with the teacher rather than spend a half hour writing and reviewing this particular letter? You may have much more flexibility than you realize. If a task is self-imposed, consider what you can do to reduce its negative (stress-producing) effects on your day.

To help you recognize some of your tasks and get you started thinking about which can be delegated and which you must do yourself, complete the following exercise. From each of the twenty typical activities for teachers, decide whether the teacher *should* do this herself, should delegate the task to another adult, or should delegate it to a student. When you have finished, be honest with yourself and see whether you can practice what you preach. If you think that certain tasks *should* be delegated to others, but find that you often end up doing them yourself, there is room for improvement.

CHART KEY

A. Teacher only should do this . . . should not be delegated.

B. This task could be delegated to a volunteer aide.

C. This task could be delegated to a student.

EFFECTIVE TIME MANAGEMENT
Helping Teachers Keep the Demands of Their Job Under Control

	A	B	C
1. Prepare a presentation for a faculty meeting.			
2. Answer a call from an irate parent.			
3. Clean up the library corner.			
4. Collect the milk money and trip money.			
5. Sort the mail and notices.			
6. Mark spelling papers.			
7. Write plans in the plan book for next week.			
8. Enter grades in the marking book.			
9. Make two phone calls regarding the class trip.			
10. Take two children to the nurse's office.			
11. Orient a new student to class.			
12. Put assignments on the board for the reading groups.			
13. Write ditto masters for reinforcement activities.			
14. Attempt a team meeting for planning.			
15. Select A-V materials for social studies unit.			
16. Review math homework papers.			
17. Order paper and supplies.			
18. Have students clean out their desks.			
19. Prepare folders for Open School Night.			
20. Collapse in a heap.			

FINDING PURPOSE AND MEANING

Have you ever noticed that educators who have interests outside of teaching seem to be more vibrant, optimistic, and full of zest — more so than those who believe they have no time for anything outside their role of teaching? That those educators seem to be more exciting, self-motivated, and self-directed than others tend to be? That's because being purposeful gives life meaning. Nothing can be as stressful as working with fellow educators (or students) who have resigned themselves to feeling powerless about their lives, or have opted to be victims, not even attempting to participate in their lives in an active and vital way.

Finding purpose and meaning is also a critical element in vibrant health, motivation, ambition, achievement, self-respect, and well-being. This is as true for students as for adults. Feeling purposeful raises the level of a student's performance in school.

The Coleman Report, a comprehensive investigation of American education, concluded that the degree to which a student felt his life had meaning and direction was the second most significant determinant (parent support was the first) of whether he met with failure or success overall in his effectiveness as a student. This correlation with school success was also more important than academic performance, class size, yearly expenditure per pupil, or level of teacher preparation. As the level of self-esteem increases, so do academic achievement scores; as self-esteem decreases, so does achievement.

A recent Gallup Poll revealed that only 25 percent of all adults feel purposeful in their work, and even fewer feel an overall satisfaction with their life! Those who did express satisfaction said they were working toward two or more goals that were important to them.

Setting and Achieving (Worthwhile) Goals

A goal is like having a map. It helps you locate the direction you should be heading so that you know where you should focus your time and energy. Of course, the first step is to determine what *is* of purpose, and then work toward accomplishing it. Just being busy doesn't necessarily mean your life has focus.

The Nine Key Goals in Life

There are nine key areas that help give meaning to life. Think about the goals you'd like to set in each of these categories and then write them down.

■ **Goals for Peace of Mind:** The search for meaning and spiritual fulfillment.

_____

_____

_____

_____

_____

_____

■ **Personal Relationships:** Goals in relationships (with students, children, colleagues, parents, friends, others).

_____

_____

_____

_____

_____

■ **Learning and Education:** What would you like to know more about?

_____

_____

_____

_____

_____

■ **Fitness:** Goals for physical fitness and overall health.

_____

_____

_____

_____

_____

■ **Work Goals:** What are your goals for productive work and career success?

_____

_____

_____

_____

_____

■ **Financial Goals:** Plans for creating enough money to do the things you want to do.

_____

_____

_____

_____

_____

■ **Leisure Time:** What activities (hobbies, sports, traveling) would you like to learn more about? To do more of?

_____

_____

_____

_____

_____

■ **Status and Respect:** To which groups do you want to belong? From whom do you want respect?

_____

_____

_____

_____

_____

■ **Others:** Goals that may not fit into the previous categories.

Guidelines for Accomplishing Your Goals

Sometimes just having goals isn't enough. What motivates you to want to achieve them? The following questions can help you determine how serious you are in accomplishing your goals.

1. Is it your goal? Have you ever bought a car because your spouse loved it and thought it "looked like you," but you didn't (but you bought it anyway!)? In the same way, you may have a goal that someone else wants you to accomplish — but it's not a priority to you. If you don't really want something, it's unlikely you'll make the commitment needed to accomplish it! You'll give up when faced with hard work. You need to "own" the goal. You must have an inner fire, a drive that says, "It's important to *me*."

2. Is the goal attainable? Do you believe you can reach your goal? Is it achievable? It doesn't mean that it has to be easy, but there has to be a better than 50-50 chance you can meet the goal. You don't want a goal that is self-defeating, one that is so difficult you almost certainly will not achieve it. At the same time your goal must offer you a challenge. There's a saying that goes, "Most people don't aim too high and miss, they aim too low and hit!" If your goal is to do at least twenty sit-ups and you can already do nineteen with no problem, what's the challenge?

3. What makes the goal worth achieving? What are the benefits? Is it worth the time and effort? When you are lecturing and you say, "Now, this next material will not be on the test, but you should know it anyway," what do your students do? Do they pay as much attention as they normally would, or do they exchange a grin with friends, sit back, and relax? They probably just kick back. They don't take the material seriously because they know they won't be tested on it. They assume there's little benefit to taking notes and paying attention.

4. Have you put your goals in writing? Writing down your goals clarifies them in your mind and helps you to get organized. It gives you a plan of attack. There's another reason to write down goals. You internalize them; you buy into *your* commitment when you put pencil to paper. If it's just in your head, you can easily forget about them. We have hundreds of thousands of thoughts daily; most are forgotten in moments. But those we take the time and effort to focus on matter more.

5. Are the deadlines realistic? Goals and deadlines seem a lot easier to reach when they are broken down into manageable tasks. Set dates for each goal, major and minor. Some dates are predetermined — school vacation dates, for example — so you simply have to adjust your schedule to taking vacations at certain times. But you can still set intermediate deadlines, such as planning ahead for an intended vacation. Having a date written down helps you get motivated to manage the task by prioritizing where and how you allocate your time. When you see you're nearing a deadline, you can push yourself just a little harder, or know when to plan downtime and playtime. And of course, when you do accomplish a goal within the deadline, you feel successful.

ACT LIKE A PROFESSIONAL

Children spend a significant amount of time during their most formative years in the school environment. We as educators have the opportunity to be a significant link in helping students develop the skills and attitudes they need for living healthy and functional lives — now and as adults. Perhaps today, more than ever before, children face a world of increasing choices and options, frontiers of limitless possibilities in every direction. This means youths have a greater need to exercise independent judgment, and to take responsibility for the choices, values, and actions that will shape their lives.

The more choices and decisions a person must make at a conscious level, whether a child or an adult, the more urgent is the need for high self-esteem. Ever-challenging and competitive, our workplaces require an unprecedentedly higher level of knowledge and skill among all participants as well as a higher level of personal autonomy, self-reliance, self-trust, self-esteem, and the capacity to exercise initiative.

There's a difference between getting a high school diploma and a meaningful education, as you and I know. When we feel we may not be preparing our students to meet the twentieth century successfully, a vague stress results. We know that our students, in addition to acquiring the skills of reading, writing, and learning, need to gain valuable *self-knowledge* and *self-respect*. We know that our students should be armed with the ability to turn their joys into their jobs, their toys into their tools — to know productive and meaningful work based on inner desires and talents. Trying to accomplish these goals places an even greater stress on those educators who want to help students but feel there isn't time to do so in the regular school curriculum.

We know what the important life skills are. Just as for us, we want our students to be capable of entering into mutually satisfying and loving relationships, those in which they will not be beaten up emotionally or physically, nor do we want them to hurt the people whom they love. We want them to be in good health and know how to sustain their body's wellness. We want them to discover the connection between self-responsibility and happiness and to care for their emotional well-being. We want them to be compassionate people, able to nurture and sustain the warmth of friendships. We want them to live a life characterized by meaning, to be able to set and achieve *worthwhile* goals. Good educators know there's a difference between doing the right things and doing things right.

HOW EFFECTIVE ARE YOU?

If you think you're an effective educator, you experience less stress than those who aren't sure that they are making a difference. Are you an effective educator? Think about the teachers you had in school — the ones you liked as well as those you didn't.

- Did some manage to involve you in the subject they were teaching and make you *want* to learn?

- Did some exude warmth and compassion?

- Did some exude vitality and excellence?

- Did certain ones make you feel that you could ask them anything you wanted about their subject?

- Did the best teachers make you think and participate in class rather than allow you to hide between the boy sitting in front of you and sneak peeks at the clock on the wall to see how much time was left in the period?

- Were some teachers so exciting that you looked forward to their classes?

- Did a few teachers even talk *with* students rather than lecture *at* them day after day?

- Did you notice that in some classes time flew by because you were busy every minute rather than playing with your pencil and day-dreaming while you waited for the class to start or the teacher to hand out and collect homework?

■ Did the best teachers treat all students as part of the class rather than ignore the slow students because they were going to do poorly and the smart ones because they could take care of themselves?

If you can answer yes to many of these questions, then you are remembering effective teachers — those who helped you get "a real education," and to learn the "real stuff."

Effective educators come in a variety of sizes and shapes, and they possess different personalities and teaching methods and styles, but they share certain characteristics. Effective educators:

■ **Don't write off any student.** Good teachers don't have one set of standards for good students and lower standards for others. They know that students learn at different rates. While some students are quicker than others, some need more help in understanding the lesson. Good teachers are convinced that *all students can learn*. These educators believe that it's their job to see that all students reach not only the course proficiency requirements, but they set high expectations for all students in helping them fulfill their potential. They know that students who are expected to do well in school usually succeed, while those who are expected to fail usually do so.

■ **Know the importance of praise as a motivator.** Effective educators don't take good behavior or success for granted, nor do they comment only on misbehavior or failure. Successful teachers continually encourage their students and provide experiences where each student can enjoy a measure of success.

■ **Create an atmosphere conducive to learning.** Warmth and enthusiasm for the subjects taught often go together. Good educators make subjects come alive and simultaneously make all students feel appreciated and cared about.

■ **Use class time well.** Good teachers have a commitment to learning, not just teaching. They develop creative and stimulating lesson plans, and through a series of teaching methodologies, test for student learning. They know that if students aren't learning, they need to find alternative ways in which the student *does* succeed in learning.

■ **Establish clear boundaries for students.** Good teachers make only those rules that are conducive to keeping students physically and emotionally safe, and they are consistent and fair when reinforcing them.

■ **Seize learning opportunities.** Good teachers encourage all of their students to contribute, and are willing to move the class in a new direction that seems to be more understandable and interesting to the students.

■ **Have a clearly defined philosophy.** Good teachers know that in order to focus on those things that are of most value, they need to have a philosophy to guide their actions.

The Role of Philosophy in Your Teaching Life

At the heart of purposeful activity in teaching is an educational philosophy that helps educators to answer value-laden questions and make decisions from among the many choices we have. A philosophy serves to provide purpose in education, to clarify objectives and activities, to suggest learning theories, to define the curriculum, and to guide the selection of strategies for teaching. It articulates what *you* want from your teaching and specifies the activities needed for working with youth. Furthermore, it defines and clarifies your role, and guides the selection of strategies that will help you accomplish that. There are many ways to teach. Curriculum decisions ultimately reflect differing beliefs and values about what we see as important values to pass on to our students.

What are your beliefs about education? Have you solidified your values so that you can make decisions for your students and for their learning? If you have, then you experience less stress than educators who have not.

Why Understanding Your Philosophy Reduces Stress

The benefits of consciously choosing a philosophy are numerous. The following list is just a beginning, and you will want to add your own thoughts. The idea is that you see the value of carefully thinking through and evaluating a philosophy that will guide your actions and enable you to be more effective (and satisfied) in your role as an educator.

■ With a philosophy I can look at ideas about teaching and determine those values I really want to impart and those I want to change.

■ Thinking about what is important to teach guides my actions.

■ I become more aware of my strengths, of how much I have to offer students, and this gives me courage and confidence to pull through the challenging times.

■ I set goals for myself as an educator so I have a concrete objective to work towards. This helps me change what I don't like about my teaching and set new standards to work toward.

■ I become more clear about what I really want for my students and what I'm actually giving each one.

■ I become more aware of my own repressed but natural resentments about teaching, such as the lack of freedom and the sacrifices, and I am then able to acknowledge these in a healthy manner.

The Search for a Philosophical Attitude

Schooling is a moral venture, one that necessitates choosing specific values from among innumerable possibilities. Each educator must face and answer some difficult questions about the purpose of schooling and about his or her role in working with students. For example:

■ What is education for?

■ What should the school accept responsibility for?

■ What kind of citizens and what kind of society do we want?

■ What methods of instruction or classroom organization must we provide to produce these desired ends?

■ Is the purpose of school to change, adapt to, or accept the social order?

■ What objectives should be common to all?

■ Should objectives deal with controversial issues or only those for which there is established knowledge?

■ Should objectives be based on the needs of society in general or the expressed needs of students?

The Five Educational Philosophies and What They Mean

There are five distinct educational philosophies: perennialism, idealism, realism, experimentalism, and existentialism. Collectively, these philosophies represent a broad spectrum of thought about what schools should be and do. Educators holding differing philosophies would create very different schools for students to attend and learn in.

1. Perennialism. The most conservative, traditional, or inflexible of the five philosophies is perennialism. Perennialists believe that education, like human nature, is a constant. Since the distinguishing characteristic of humans is the ability to reason, education should focus on developing rationality: Education is a preparation for life, and students should be taught the world's permanencies through structured study. Perennialists would favor a curriculum of subjects taught through highly disciplined drills and behavior control. The teacher interprets and tells. The student is a passive recipient.

2. Idealism. This philosophy espouses that *reality* is a world within a person's mind. Goodness as an ideal state is something to be striven for. Teachers would be models of ideal behavior whose job would be to sharpen their students' intellectual processes. Students in such schools would have a somewhat passive role, receiving and memorizing the reporting of the teacher. Change in the school program would generally be considered an intrusion on the orderly process of educating.

3. Realism. Change is a natural evolution; the world is as it is, and the job of schools would be to teach students about the world. The realist would favor a school dominated by subjects of the here-and-now world, such as math and science. Students would be taught factual information for mastery. The teacher would impart knowledge of this reality to students. Classrooms would be highly ordered and disciplined, like nature, and the students would be possible participants in the curriculum. Changes in school would be perceived as a natural evolution toward a perfection of order.

4. Experimentalism. The experimentalist openly accepts change, for the world is an ever-changing place. Reality is what is actually experienced; truth is what presently functions; good-

ness is what is accepted by public test. Unlike the perennialist, idealist, and realist, the experimentalist openly accepts change and continually seeks to discover new ways to expand and improve society. The experimentalist would favor a school with heavy emphasis on social subjects and experiences. Learning would occur through a problem-solving or inquiry format. Teachers would aid or consult with learners actively involved in discovering and experiencing the world in which they live. Such an education program would focus on value development in terms of group rather than individual consequences.

5. Existentialism. The existentialist feels that change is natural and necessary. For existentialists, schools, if they existed at all, would be places that assisted students in knowing themselves and learning of their place in society. If subject matter existed, it would be a matter of interpretation, such as the arts, ethics, or philosophy. Teacher-student interaction would center around assisting students in their personal learning journeys. Change in school environments would be embraced as both a natural and necessary phenomenon.

Classroom space, organization and dissemination of knowledge, uses of learning materials, instructional style, teaching strategies, organization of students, discipline, and student roles are all indicators of your philosophy. This philosophy is an indicator of how you do a number of things. For example, your philosophy or beliefs about schools and students reveals your values. What do *you* believe? What is your philosophy? Here's a self-assessment to help you examine your preferred educational philosophy.

Philosophy Preference Assessment

© Jon Wiles, Joseph C. Bondi, 1984. Reprinted with permission.

DIRECTIONS: For each item below, respond according to the strength of your belief, scoring the item on a scale of 1 to 5. A one (1) indicates strong disagreement, a five (5) indicates strong agreement.

1 2 3 4 5   **(1)** Ideal teachers are constant questioners.

1 2 3 4 5   **(2)** Schools exist for societal improvement.

1 2 3 4 5   **(3)** Teaching should center around the inquiry technique.

1 2 3 4 5   **(4)** Demonstration and recitation are essential components of learning.

1 2 3 4 5   **(5)** Students should always be permitted to determine their own rules in the educational process.

1 2 3 4 5   **(6)** Reality is spiritual and rational.

1 2 3 4 5   **(7)** Curriculum should be based on the laws of natural science.

1 2 3 4 5   **(8)** The teacher should be a strong authority figure in the classroom.

1 2 3 4 5   **(9)** The student is a receiver of knowledge.

1 2 3 4 5   **(10)** Ideal teachers interpret knowledge.

1 2 3 4 5   **(11)** Lecture-discussion is the most effective teaching technique.

1 2 3 4 5   **(12)** Institutions should seek avenues towards self-improvement through an orderly process.

1 2 3 4 5   **(13)** Schools are obligated to teach moral truths.

1 2 3 4 5   **(14)** School programs should focus on social problems and issues.

1 2 3 4 5   **(15)** Institutions exist to preserve and strengthen spiritual and social values.

1 2 3 4 5   **(16)** Subjective opinion reveals truth.

1 2 3 4 5   **(17)** Teachers are seen as facilitators of learning.

1 2 3 4 5   **(18)** Schools should be educational "smorgasbords."

1 2 3 4 5   **(19)** Memorization is the key to process skills.

1 2 3 4 5   **(20)** Reality consists of objects.

1 2 3 4 5   **(21)** Schools exist to foster the intellectual process.

1 2 3 4 5   **(22)** Schools foster an orderly means for change.

1 2 3 4 5   **(23)** There are essential skills everyone must learn.

1 2 3 4 5   **(24)** Teaching by subject area is the most effective approach.

1 2 3 4 5   **(25)** Students should play an active part in program design and evaluation.

1 2 3 4 5   **(26)** A functioning member of society follows rules of conduct.

1 2 3 4 5 **(27)** Reality is rational.

1 2 3 4 5 **(28)** Schools should reflect the society they serve.

1 2 3 4 5 **(29)** The teacher should set an example for the students.

1 2 3 4 5 **(30)** The most effective learning does not take place in a highly structured, strictly disciplined environment.

1 2 3 4 5 **(31)** The curriculum should be based on unchanging spiritual truths.

1 2 3 4 5 **(32)** The most effective learning is nonstructured.

1 2 3 4 5 **(33)** Truth is a constant expressed through ideas.

1 2 3 4 5 **(34)** Drill and factual knowledge are important components of any learning environment.

1 2 3 4 5 **(35)** Societal consensus determines morality.

1 2 3 4 5 **(36)** Knowledge is gained primarily through the senses.

1 2 3 4 5 **(37)** There are essential pieces of knowledge that everyone should know.

1 2 3 4 5 **(38)** The school exists to facilitate self-awareness.

1 2 3 4 5 **(39)** Change is an ever-present process.

1 2 3 4 5 **(40)** Truths are best taught through the inquiry process.

Philosophy Assessment Scoring

The following sets of questions relate to the five standard philosophies of education:

Perennialist: 6, 8, 10, 13, 15, 31, 34, 37

Idealist: 9, 11, 19, 21, 24, 27, 29, 33

Realist: 4, 7, 12, 20, 22, 23, 26, 28

Experimentalist: 2, 3, 14, 17, 25, 35, 39, 40

Existentialist: 1, 5, 16, 18, 30, 32, 36, 38

Scoring Steps

1. Taking these questions by set (e.g., the eight perennialist questions), record the value of the answer given (i.e., Strongly Disagree =1). Total the numerical value of each set. In a single set of numbers, the total should fall between 8 (all 1's) and 40 (all 5's).

2. Divide the total score for each set by five (example 40/5 = 8).

3. Plot the scores.

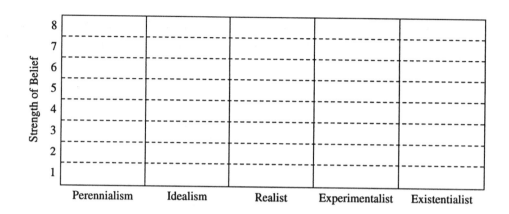

Interpretation

Having plotted your responses on the grid, you now have a profile which will give you an idea of your beliefs about schools. Some patterns are common and therefore subject to interpretation.

Pattern #1. If your profile on the response grid is basically flat, reflecting approximately the same score for each set of questions, it indicates an inability to discriminate in terms of preference.

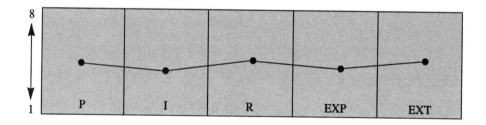

Pattern #2. If your pattern is generally a slanting line across the grid, then you show a strong structured or nonstructured orientation in your reported beliefs.

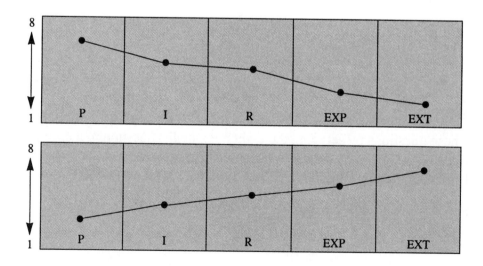

Pattern #3. If your pattern appears as a bimodal or trimodal distribution (two or three peaks), it indicates indecisiveness on crucial issues and suggests the need for further clarification. The closer the peaks (adjacent sets), the less contradiction in the responses.

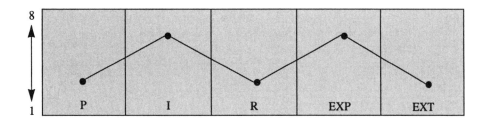

Pattern #4. If the pattern appears U-shaped, a significant amount of value inconsistency is indicated. Such a response would suggest strong beliefs in very different and divergent systems.

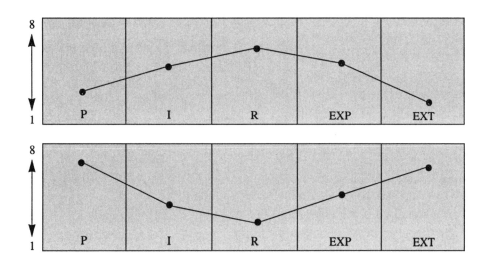

Pattern #5. A pattern which is simply a flowing curve without sharp peaks and valleys may suggest either an eclectic philosophy or a person only beginning to study his or her own philosophy.

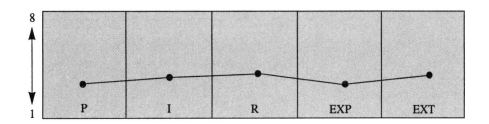

DIET AND NUTRITION

Can you list what you had to eat today? What did you have for dinner yesterday? When was the last time you had proteins, carbohydrates, and a full complement of vitamins and minerals all in one meal?

When you are under time and stress pressures, your need for certain nutrients increases. You may find yourself eating more as you work longer hours; your body is indicating its needs. By keeping track of your diet and nutrition, you can more accurately chart when you are meeting those needs and when a lack of good nutrition can be adding to your stress. The goal is to find out what works for *you*.

Diet and nutrition contribute to good health and play an important role in alleviating stress. As health experts say, "We are what we eat." Good health depends on a balanced diet. A deficiency of certain vitamins, minerals, and nutrients can upset body chemistry. Any diet that emphasizes one type of food (proteins, vegetables, carbohydrates) to the exclusion of other foods may be very harmful to the body.

When the body is deprived of basic nourishment, resulting in a deficiency of essential nutrients, it's even less capable of withstanding the effects of stress, and even more susceptible to major health breakdowns. For example, brain cells, like the rest of the body, require proper feeding in order to function correctly. The brain is the body's most chemically sensitive organ. Recent studies indicate that excessive sugar, vitamin deficiencies, and food allergies can seriously disrupt the brain's ability to function normally and effectively.

The U.S. Senate Committee on Nutrition and Human Needs has established the following dietary goals for balanced nutrition:

1. Consume only as many calories as are expended. If overweight, decrease caloric consumption and increase physical activity.

2. Increase the intake of complex carbohydrates and natural sugars from about 28% to about 48% of total calories consumed.

3. Reduce the intake of refined and processed sugars to account for no more than 10% of total caloric consumption.

4. Reduce overall fat intake from approximately 40% to about 30% of caloric consumption.

5. Reduce saturated fat intake to account for about 10% of total caloric consumption. Balance it with polyunsaturated and mono-unsaturated fats, each of which should also account for about 10% of caloric consumption.

6. Reduce cholesterol consumption to about 300 milligrams a day.

7. Limit the intake of sodium by reducing the intake of salt to about 5 grams a day.

These goals suggest the following changes in food selection and preparation:

1. Increase consumption of fruits, vegetables, and whole grains.

2. Decrease consumption of refined and other processed sugars and foods high in such sugars.

3. Decrease consumption of foods high in total fat, and partially replace saturated fats, whether obtained from animal or vegetable sources, with polyunsaturated fats.

4. Decrease consumption of animal fat and choose lean meats, poultry, and fish.

5. Substitute low-fat and nonfat milk for whole milk and low-fat dairy products for high-fat dairy products.

6. Decrease consumption of butterfat, eggs, and other high-cholesterol foods.

7. Decrease consumption of salt and of foods with a high salt content.

Good dietary habits begin with breakfast. If you're like most adults, you preach the importance of having breakfast to your own children and to your students, but then maybe skip it yourself. Yet, proper nourishment is so important to managing the day at hand. Just as you can't get your car around the block without gas, you can't have use of the brain's capabilities if it hasn't been fueled. Breakfast should consist of fruits and grains that will steadily release glucose during the day, giving fuel to the brain. The vital nutrients are the following:

Protein: Protein is required to maintain and repair body tissues, to make hemoglobin (which carries oxygen to the cells), to form antibodies to fight off infection and disease, and to produce enzymes and hormones to regulate body processes. To a lesser extent, it is required for energy.

Carbohydrates: Essentially, when we talk about carbohydrates in the diet, we mean sugars, starches, and indigestible materials such as cellulose. Starches are complex forms of glucose. Both forms are broken down by digestion into blood sugar, the glucose in the blood. The main source of energy for the red blood cells and the central nervous system, glucose also functions to spare protein from being used for energy, thus freeing that substance for more important functions, such as tissue growth and repair.

Fat: In addition to being a concentrated dietary source of energy, fat supplies an essential fatty acid and carries vitamins A, D, E, and K. Deposits of fat in certain areas of the body serve to support and cushion vital organs and provide insulation. Triglycerides are the most common form of fat in the body. Elevated levels of triglycerides often occur in persons with prolonged symptoms of the stress response. However, these break down into fatty acids, which are essential to the body's functions.

Vitamin A: This vitamin has an important role in the building of body cells. It maintains the function of mucous membranes, which form the inner linings of the gastrointestinal and respiratory tracts. Vitamin A is also essential in preventing certain eye diseases which may lead to blindness.

Thiamine (Vitamin B1): This vitamin has a role in the body's enzyme systems. Essentially, it helps release energy during the oxidation of carbohydrates. It also helps to maintain healthy nerves and a normal appetite and digestion and plays a role in growth processes. Because it is water-soluble, excessive levels of this vitamin are eliminated. For this reason, it must be replenished frequently.

Riboflavin (Vitamin B2): This vitamin functions in the enzyme systems also. It has roles in growth processes as well as in the maintenance of healthy skin and mucous membranes. It is concentrated mostly in the liver and kidneys. Like Vitamin B1, it also needs replenishing because the body does not store it well.

Niacin: This vitamin functions in the enzyme action of sugar breakdown and in the synthesis of fats. It is essential to the maintenance of healthy skin, mouth and tongue, and digestive-tract function. It is also important to nerve functioning. It is water-soluble and not stored in great amounts by the body.

Vitamin C: Its primary role is in the formation and maintenance of collagen, the vital substance which binds body cells together.

Vitamin D: This vitamin is essential to bone and tooth health. Like Vitamin A, it is fat-soluble and stored very well in the body. For this reason, it is important to avoid overdosage, which can be very dangerous.

Calcium: It is essential to the formation of new bone and for the maintenance of good bone structure and density. It is also vital to healthy nerves, heart, and muscle action.

Iron: Blood contains most of the three to five grams of iron that the body usually carries. The iron is absorbed by the intestinal tract and transported to bone marrow. Combined with protein, it makes hemoglobin, the red substance in red blood cells. Iron also functions in the enzyme systems in combination with other substances.

Your body cannot function properly when it lacks essential nutrients. In all, the body needs about 47 different nutritional substances to sustain its internal chemistry. Nutritionists agree that eating a balanced diet is the best way to get the proper mix of nutrients, but vitamin supplementation is frequently needed to replace the supply of nutrients robbed by the effects of pollutants and to help maintain the body's natural defense against stress.

Vitamins can help improve general resistance to stress and illness. For example, Vitamin B complex, magnesium, potassium, and calcium folate provide relief from fatigue and depression. The best advice when it comes to vitamin supplementation is this: A balanced diet should provide all the essential vitamins and nutrients, but taking a one-a-day vitamin tablet that contains all the essential vitamins and nutrients is also a good idea. All other doses and megadoses of single vitamins and nutrients should be taken only on the advice of a physician.

The *Daily Diet and Nutrition Log* on the next page will help you monitor your nutritional habits. Simply record your food intake. After you've monitored your nutritional habits for about a month, you may wish to visit a nutritionist (have your family doctor recommend one) to see if your food intake is sufficient for your body for sustaining you in your lifestyle.

FITNESS AND EXERCISE

Getting adequate exercise, in addition to eating a proper diet, is an effective way to combat stress. Many of us don't get sufficient physical nutrition. All too often, the demands on our time and the multiplicity of our roles leave us with little time or energy for getting the proper amount of exercise required for good health, or so we think. Unfortunately, exercise or physical fitness seems to be the first area we ignore when our schedule gets hectic. However, the opposite should be true: In times of stress, we should increase physical activity. The benefits of exercise include:

- Increased circulation
- Assistance to the heart
- Added oxygen to the body
- Improved digestion
- Relaxed nerves, balanced emotions
- Increased resistance to disease
- Reduced fatigue
- Strengthened muscles, bones, and ligaments
- Improved figure and complexion
- Sharpened mental powers

These benefits speak for themselves. You can take an active role in increasing your fitness through exercise. Here are some suggestions.

1. Think Fitness. If you are fit, stay fit. If you feel that you need to work on fitness, perhaps it's time for you to get active again. Group activities are an easy way to begin. Saturdays and Sundays are a good time for outings, especially if your week is crowded and excludes opportunities for exercise. Going to the beach, camping, hiking, and bicycling can be a regular part of your time with family and friends. "Working at playing" is one way to make fitness a total part of your health routine.

Daily Diet and Nutrition Log

DATE____

	BREAKFAST		LUNCH		DINNER		SNACKS
MONDAY	1		1		1		
	2		2		2		
	3		3		3		
	4		4		4		
TUESDAY	1		1		1		
	2		2		2		
	3		3		3		
	4		4		4		
WEDNESDAY	1		1		1		
	2		2		2		
	3		3		3		
	4		4		4		
THURSDAY	1		1		1		
	2		2		2		
	3		3		3		
	4		4		4		
FRIDAY	1		1		1		
	2		2		2		
	3		3		3		
	4		4		4		
SATURDAY	1		1		1		
	2		2		2		
	3		3		3		
	4		4		4		
SUNDAY	1		1		1		
	2		2		2		
	3		3		3		
	4		4		4		

2. Challenge Exercise. Get involved in activities where you can channel the need for risk, adventure, and challenge in a productive and positive way. If you have had it with calisthenics, which do not necessarily do much for the cardiovascular system anyway, an alternative is a new fitness concept called Challenge Exercise (CE). CE adds the element of challenge to physical fitness. Challenge adds the bonus of mental well-being to the well-known euphoric experience of exercise, resulting in a degree of well-being rarely experienced after a non-challenge exercise. It is believed that this experience (rather than the fact that exercise is good for the body) is what causes participants to continually return to CE sports rather than give in and let the demands of a busy schedule take priority over wellness.

Examples of CE sports are swimming, skiing, surfing, horseback riding, motorcycling, bicycling, mountain and rock climbing, scuba diving, and other activities that combine a high degree of physical and mental coordination. (Non-CE sports are those such as calisthenics, jogging, or a game of golf with a motor cart.) Because it benefits both mind and body, CE provides an excellent means of reducing stress.

3. Team Sports. Team sports provide you with an opportunity to stay fit and have fun. Interacting with others allows you to do a lot of laughing and shouting, which releases some of your aggression and lessens stress. It would be a little odd for you to yell at the top of your lungs while jogging alone; doing so during group activities is encouraged and is a great way to blow off steam.

4. Build Fitness Slowly and Regularly. The essential component of any effective health program is that it be aerobic in nature. Physical endurance doesn't rely solely upon strong muscles. In other words, aerobic exercises build the body's organs naturally in order to do the body's natural work.

Aerobic exercise requires you to exert a good deal of effort, but doesn't consume oxygen faster than your heart and lungs can supply it. Experts recommend three sessions of vigorous activity weekly, with each session lasting from twenty to thirty minutes. These can include walking, swimming, bicycling, aerobics, jazzercise, and so on. Remember, however, to start off slowly if you're not in shape. Pick up your pace and raise your expectations as your body adjusts to your regimen.

Before planning your program of regular physical exercise, however, you should see your own doctor. You should have a thorough physical examination before you embark on an exercise program of any kind. Your doctor will tell you, based upon your physical condition, just how vigorous your exercise can be.

You are probably convinced of the advantages of exercise and have known all along that you need to get your heart pumping a little stronger. But you may think — possibly erroneously — that you already get enough exercise just chasing around after the kids and dodging the teacher across the hall who always wants to borrow your projector. You can start your assessment by completing the *Daily Exercise and Fitness Log*. Use these guidelines for completing it.

- *Aerobic Exercise:* (walking, swimming, bicycling, running)
- *Non-Aerobic Exercise:* (weight lifting, floor exercises)
- *Sports and Games:* (volleyball, golf, bowling)
- *Others:* (other activities you feel provide exercise)

Daily Exercise and Fitness Log

DATE____

	AEROBIC EXERCISE		NON-AEROBIC EXERCISE		SPORTS AND GAMES		OTHERS
MONDAY	1 2 3 4	1 2 3 4	1 2 3 4	1 2 3 4	1 2 3 4	1 2 3 4	
TUESDAY	1 2 3 4	1 2 3 4	1 2 3 4	1 2 3 4	1 2 3 4	1 2 3 4	
WEDNESDAY	1 2 3 4	1 2 3 4	1 2 3 4	1 2 3 4	1 2 3 4	1 2 3 4	
THURSDAY	1 2 3 4	1 2 3 4	1 2 3 4	1 2 3 4	1 2 3 4	1 2 3 4	
FRIDAY	1 2 3 4	1 2 3 4	1 2 3 4	1 2 3 4	1 2 3 4	1 2 3 4	
SATURDAY	1 2 3 4	1 2 3 4	1 2 3 4	1 2 3 4	1 2 3 4	1 2 3 4	
SUNDAY	1 2 3 4	1 2 3 4	1 2 3 4	1 2 3 4	1 2 3 4	1 2 3 4	

YOUR HEALTH PROFILE
How Healthy Is Your Lifestyle?

How much time do you take to just contemplate what's going on in your life? Get into the practice of building into your lifestyle the habit of taking regular periods of time for self-evaluation, with the starting point an open-ended contemplation of where you have been and where you would like to go. Sit quietly for a while with the deliberate intention of sorting out the myriad demands, calls to duty, perceived necessities, and time constraints which flood your consciousness with a depressing sense of urgency and priority. In repose, contemplation, meditation, or whatever name you give it, false pressures dissipate and the essential priorities fall into order.

Your lifestyle, your day-to-day life, plays an important part in your well-being and stress resilience. How healthy is your lifestyle? The following profile can give you a general idea.

INTRUCTIONS

Circle only the answers that apply to you, either on the left, in the center, or on the right.

The plus and minus signs next to some numbers indicate more than (+) and less than (—).

TO SCORE: Give yourself **1 point** for each answer in column 1; **3 points** for each answer in column 2; **5 points** for each answer in column 3.

EXERCISE

Physical effort expended during the workday is mostly?

Heavy labor	Light work	Deskwork
1	3	5

Participation in physical activities (skiing, golf, swimming, etc., or lawn mowing, gardening, etc.)?

Daily	Weekly	Seldom
1	3	5

Participation in a vigorous exercise program?

3 Times Weekly	Weekly	Seldom
1	3	5

Average miles walked or jogged per day?

1 or More	Less Than 1	None
1	3	5

Flights of stairs climbed per day?

10 Plus	Fewer Than 10
1	3

NUTRITION

Are you overweight?

No	5 to 9 lbs.	20+ lbs.
1	3	5

Do you eat a variety from each of the following five food groups: (1) meat, fish, poultry, dried legumes, eggs or nuts; (2) milk or milk products; (3) bread or cereals; (4) fruits; (5) vegetables?

Each Day	3 Times Weekly
1	3

ALCOHOL

Average number of bottles (12 oz.) of beer per week?

0 to 7	8 to 15	16+
1	3	5

Average number of hard liquor (1½ oz.) drinks per week?

0 to 7	8 to 15	16+
1	3	5

Average number of glasses (5 oz.) of wine or beer per week?

0 to 7	8 to 15	16+
1	3	5

Total number of drinks per week, including beer, liquor, and wine?

0 to 7	8 to 15	16+
1	3	5

DRUGS

Do you take drugs illegally?

No	Yes
1	5

Do you consume alcoholic beverages together with certain drugs (tranquilizers, barbiturates, illegal drugs)?

No	Yes
1	5

Do you use pain-killers improperly or excessively?

No	Yes
1	5

TOBACCO

Cigarettes smoked per day?

None	Fewer Than 10	10+
1	3	5

Cigars smoked per day?

None	Fewer Than 10	10+
1	3	5

Pipe tobacco pouches per week?

None	Fewer Than 10	10+
1	3	5

PERSONAL HEALTH

Do you experience periods of depression?

Seldom	Occasionally	Frequently
1	3	5

Does anxiety interfere with your daily activities?

Seldom	Occasionally	Frequently
1	3	5

Do you get enough satisfying sleep?

Yes	No
1	3

Are you aware of the causes and danger of VD?

Yes	No
1	3

Breast self-examination? (If not applicable, do not score.)

Monthly	Occasionally
1	3

ROAD AND WATER SAFETY

Mileage per year as driver or passenger?

Less than 10,000	More than 10,000
1	3

Do you exceed the speed limit?

No	By 10 mph+	By 20 mph+
1	3	5

Do you wear a seat belt?

Always	Occasionally	Never
1	3	5

Do you drive a motorcycle, moped, or snowmobile?

No	Yes
1	3

If yes to the above, do you always wear a regulation safety helmet?

Yes		No
1	3	5

Do you ever drive under the influence of alcohol?

Never	Occasionally
1	5

Do you ever drive when your ability may be affected by drugs?

Never	Occasionally
1	5

Are you aware of water-safety rules?

Yes	No
1	3

GENERAL

Average time watching TV per day (in hours)?

0 to 1	1 to 4	4+
1	3	5

Are you familiar with first-aid procedures?

Yes	No
1	3

Do you ever smoke in bed?

No	Occasionally	Yes
1	3	5

Do you always make use of equipment provided for your safety at work?

Yes	Occasionally	No
1	3	5

TOTAL SCORE_____
(Add up your circled numbers.)

HOW TO CALCULATE YOUR SCORE

Excellent   34—45

You have a commendable lifestyle based on sensible habits and a lively awareness of personal health.

Good   46—55

With some minor changes you can develop an excellent lifestlyle.

Risky   56—65

You are taking unnecessary risks with your health. Several of your habits should be changed if potential health problems are to be avoided.

Hazardous   66 and over

Either you have little personal awareness of good health habits, or you are choosing to ignore them. This is a danger zone.

How did you do? Were you surprised at your score? Are you as robust as you'd like to be? If your score is less than you'd like it to be, use that information to motivate yourself.

RELAXATION TECHNIQUES TO REDUCE STRESS

When you relax your body, you relax your state of mind. When you control your breathing, you're directing your body through your mind. Conscious relaxation is a very effective method for eliminating tension, enabling you to ward off stress, or when experiencing the stress response, to reduce its discomforts and offset damaging effects.

It doesn't take an enormous amount of time to learn to release the tension in your muscles and acquire more energy. There are several ways you can achieve this.

Progressive Muscle Relaxation

This technique uses physical exercise to achieve relaxation from tension. It can also be used for alleviating a number of disorders including anxiety, insomnia, headaches, back-aches, and hypertension. The state of physical relaxation produced is pleasant and allows you to feel rested and refreshed. Some people shy away from this form of relaxation, thinking that they might lose motivation or become sluggish, a particularly negative effect if you're in the middle of a busy day. However, this is not the case — they do not become lazy, bored, or tired. In fact, just the opposite occurs. By using progressive relaxation, they can remain alert, avoid fatigue, and restore vitality.

This technique gets its name because each muscle group is tensed and relaxed individually, slowly progressing throughout the body. Tensing and relaxing the muscles helps you to increase your awareness of the body's muscular response to stress. Think for a moment about the last time you were really upset and tense. No doubt your legs were in a defensive stance, your jaw was set tight, your eyes were glaring intensely. Chances are your muscles stayed tense long after the stressful event.

Using progressive muscle relaxation as a form of de-stressing doesn't take very long, about fifteen minutes. Here are the principles:

Find a quiet location free of interruptions and dim the lights. You may practice this exercise while reclining on a sofa, or sitting in a comfortable chair (preferably one that reclines — it's easier to learn the exercise the first time while reclining). Later, it will be beneficial to practice while sitting up or standing. This exercise is most effective if you follow the word-by-word script provided below. Record the script yourself so that it's available for use at any time. Add your favorite soothing music as a background. Here's the word-by-word script.

[For Total Body Tension.] "First, tense every muscle in your body. Tense the muscles of your jaw, eyes, arms, hands, chest, back, stomach, legs, and feet. Feel the tension all over your body . . . Hold the tension briefly, and then relax and let go as you breathe out. . . Let your whole body relax. . . Feel a wave of calm come over you as you stop tensing.

"Take another deep breath . . . Study the tension as you hold your breath . . . Slowly breathe out and relax and let go. Feel the deepening relaxation. Allow yourself to drift more and more with this relaxation . . . As you continue, you will exercise different parts of your body. Become aware of your body, and its tension and relaxation. This will help you to become deeply relaxed."

[Head and Face.] "Keeping the rest of your body relaxed, wrinkle up your forehead. Do you feel the tension? Your forehead is very tight. Briefly pause and be aware of it . . . Now relax and let go. Feel the tension slipping out. Smooth our your forehead and take a deep breath. Hold it briefly. Breathe out, and relax.

"Squint your eyes. Keep the rest of your body relaxed. Briefly pause and feel the tension around your eyes. Take a deep breath and hold it. Breathe out, and relax.

"Open your mouth as wide as you can. Feel the tension in your jaw and chin. Briefly hold the tension. Now let your mouth gently close. Relax and let go. Take a deep breath. Hold it. As you breathe out, relax and let go.

"Close your mouth. Push your tongue against the roof of your mouth. Study the tension in your mouth and chin. Briefly hold the tension . . . Relax. Take a deep breath. Hold it. Now relax and let go as you breathe out. When you breathe out, let your tongue rest comfortably in your mouth, and let your lips be slightly apart.

"Keep the rest of your body relaxed but clench your jaw tightly. Feel the tension in your jaw muscles. Briefly hold the tension . . . Now relax and let go. Take a deep breath. Hold it. Again, relax and let go as you breathe out.

"Think about the top of your head, your forehead, eyes, jaws, and cheeks. Make sure these muscles are relaxed . . . Have you let go of all the tension? Continue to let the tension slip away and feel the relaxation replace the tension. Feel your face becoming very smooth and soft as all the tension slips away . . . Your eyes are relaxed . . . Your tongue is relaxed. Your jaws are loose and limp . . . All of your neck muscles are also very, very relaxed.

"All of the muscles of your face and head are relaxing more and more. Your head feels as though it could roll from side to side."

[Shoulders.] "Now shrug your shoulders up and try to touch your ears with your shoulders. Feel the tension in the shoulders and neck. Hold the tension . . . Now relax and let go. Take a deep breath. Hold it. Relax and let go as you slowly breathe out.

"Notice the difference, how the tension is giving way to relaxation. Shrug your right shoulder up and try to touch your right ear. Feel the tension in your right shoulder and along the right side of your neck. Hold the tension. Now, relax and let go. Take a deep breath. Hold it. Relax and let go as you slowly breathe out.

"Next, shrug your left shoulder up and try to touch your left ear. Feel the tension in your left shoulder and along the left side of your neck. Hold the tension. Now, relax and let go. Take a deep breath. Hold it. Relax and let go as you slowly breathe out. Feel the relaxation seeping into your shoulders. As you continue, you will become loose, limp, and as relaxed as a beanbag."

[Arms and Hands.] "Stretch your arms out and make your hands into fists. Feel the tension in your hands and forearms. Hold the tension. Hold, relax and let go. Take a deep breath. Hold it. Relax and let go as you slowly breathe out.

"Push your right hand down into the surface it is resting on. Feel the tension in your arm and shoulder. Hold the tension . . . Now relax and let go. Take a deep breath. Hold it. Relax and let go as you slowly breathe out.

"Next, push your left hand down into whatever it is resting on. Feel the tension in your arm and shoulder. Hold the tension . . . Now relax and let go. Take a deep breath. Hold it. Relax and let go as you slowly breathe out.

"Bend your arms toward your shoulders and double them up as you would do to show off your muscles. Feel the tension. Hold the tension . . . Now relax and let go. Take a deep breath. Hold it. Relax and let go as you slowly breathe out."

[Chest and Lungs.] "Move on to the relaxation of your chest. Begin by taking a deep breath that totally fills your lungs. As you hold your breath, notice the tension. Be aware of the tension around your ribs . . . Relax and let go as you slowly breathe out. Feel the deepening relaxation as you continue breathing easily, freely, and gently.

"Take in another deep breath. Hold it and again feel the contrast between tension and relaxation. As you do, tighten your chest muscles. Hold the tension. Relax and let go as you slowly breathe out. Feel the relief as you breathe out. Continue to breathe gently. Breathe as smoothly as you can. You will become more and more relaxed with every breath."

[Back.] "Keep your face, neck, arms, and chest as relaxed as possible. Arch your back up (or forward, if you are sitting). Arch it as though you had a pillow under the middle and lower parts of your back. Observe the tension along both sides of your back. Briefly hold that position. Now relax and let go. Take a deep breath. Hold it. Relax and let go as you breathe out. Let that relaxation spread deep into your shoulders and down into your back muscles.

"Feel the slow relaxation developing and spreading all over. Feel it going deeper and deeper. Allow your entire body to relax. Face and head relaxed . . . Neck relaxed . . . Shoulders relaxed . . . Arms relaxed . . . Chest relaxed . . . Back relaxed . . . All these areas are relaxing more and more, becoming more deeply relaxed."

[Stomach.] "Now begin the relaxation of the stomach area. Tighten up this area. Briefly hold the tension . . . Relax and let go. Feel the relaxation pour into your stomach area. All the tension is being replaced with relaxation. Take a deep breath. Hold it. Relax and let go as you slowly breathe out.

"Now experience a different type of tension in the stomach area. Push your stomach out as far as you can. Briefly hold the tension . . . Now relax and let go. Take a deep breath. Hold it. Relax and let go as you slowly breathe out. Now pull your stomach in. Try to pull your stomach in and touch your backbone. Hold it . . . Now relax and let go. Take a deep breath. Hold it. Relax and let go as you breathe out.

"You are becoming more and more relaxed. Each time you breathe out, feel the gentle relaxation in your lungs and in your body."

[Hips, Legs, and Feet.] "Begin the relaxation of your hips and legs. Tighten your hips and legs by pressing down the heels of your feet into the surface they are resting on. Tighten these muscles. Keep the rest of your body as relaxed as you can and press your heels down . . . Now hold the tension . . . Relax and let go. Your legs feel as if they could float up. Take a deep breath. Hold it. Relax and let go as you slowly breathe out. Feel the relaxation pouring in.

"Next tighten your lower leg muscles. Feel the tension. Briefly hold the tension . . . Now relax and let go. Take a deep breath. Hold it. Relax and let go as you breathe out.

"Now curl your toes downward. Curl them down and try to touch the bottom of your feet with your toes. Hold them and feel the tension . . . Relax and let go. Wiggle your toes gently as you let go of the tension. Take a deep breath. Hold it. Relax and let go as you breathe out.

"Bend your toes back the other way. Bend your toes right up toward your knees. Feel the tension. Try to touch your knees with your toes. Feel the tension. Hold the tension . . . Relax and let go. Feel all the tension vanish. Take a deep breath. Hold it. Relax and let go as you slowly breathe out. Feel the tension leaving your body and the relaxation seeping in.

"You have progressed through all the major muscles of your body. Notice the difference between tension and relaxation. Now, let your muscles become more and more relaxed. Continue to feel yourself becoming more and more relaxed each time you breathe out. Your whole body is becoming more and more relaxed with each breath. Enjoy the relaxation."

[End of exercise.]

This form of relaxation can be used at anytime — to unwind after a long tense day, or to calm down before going to bed when you're feeling particularly excited or keyed up — but you needn't wait until you get home to use it. When at school — during that particularly long, tension-filled day, for example — close the door to your classroom during a break (planning period or at lunch time) and turn on your tape recorder. Again, allow about ten to fifteen minutes.

After using this technique as a way to interrupt or ward off stress, notice how you feel. During the first two weeks of practicing this skill, check for signs your body is giving you to indicate you are tense. To look for cues that your body is tensing up, ask yourself these questions: Is my forehead wrinkled? Are my jaw muscles tight? Is my stomach knotted up? Are my fists clenched?

Tensing and relaxing muscles helps you to increase your awareness of your body's muscular response to stress. Learn to use the relaxation to replace tension.

Relaxation Through Music

You can also use soothing music (very effective when combined with the progressive relaxation technique) to de-stress. As you're listening to comforting and calming sounds, take note of how your body and mind become calm and relaxed.

Also notice how the body and mind react to different kinds of music. The National Music Association (NMA) has compiled a catalogue listing of highly relaxing and meditative soothing music to bring about body and muscular relaxation. This list can be found in most major music stores.

Diaphragmatic Breathing

Controlling and regulating your breathing is another effective way to relax. When you take in air, your diaphragm expands and tenses. As you let the air out, or exhale, it relaxes. Diaphragmatic breathing encourages you to use your full capacity for breathing, by filling the lungs entirely with air, then letting go in a long, slow exhalation. Breathing correctly will help you achieve body relaxation and thereby reduce your stress level.

Many people do not know how to breathe properly. If you observe closely, you may notice yourself breathing with the chest, in short shallow breaths. This type of breathing (thoracic breathing) is thought to be indicative of unrecognized tension. It may also be detrimental to health, as it causes stale and unused air to be detained in the lungs. The healthy way to breathe is through diaphragmatic, or belly, breathing. This is the way that babies and animals breathe. It is also the proper way to breathe for achieving body relaxation. Notice your actions throughout the day. Occasionally you may sit back, stretch, and sigh deeply. In doing so, you fill the lungs and the diaphragm completely with air and then let it all out slowly. This is your body's natural way of breathing. Here are the basic principles:

1. **Inhale deeply**. First fill the diaphragm area with air (stomach goes out). Continue inhaling as the lower part of the chest expands. Finish inhaling as the upper ribs are expanded and the top of the lungs fill with air.

2. **Exhale slowly.** The air flows out smoothly from the top of the chest, down through the middle, and completely out as the stomach draws in.

3. **Rest.** Allow yourself to experience the physical sensations that accompany breathing in this relaxing manner. Begin the process again by inhaling deeply.

Here's how to achieve relaxation through proper breathing. Find a quiet place where there are no distractions. Lie down on the floor. Get as comfortable as possible. Move your arms and legs around to loosen your muscles.

1. Close your eyes.
2. Place your hands very lightly on your abdomen just below the navel with your fingertips touching.
3. Take a deep breath in and count slowly: "One . . . two . . . three . . . four." As you inhale through your nose, your abdomen should swell out. This may feel a bit awkward at first if you are used to more shallow chest breathing. You may have to make a conscious effort to push your stomach. An alternative method for checking to see whether you are using your diaphragm properly is to make a "bridge" by placing a book on your abdomen. When you inhale, you should see the lower end tilting higher.
4. After inhaling deeply, begin to exhale through the nose. Let the air out very slowly, counting one . . . two . . . three . . . four. Draw in the stomach so that your fingertips come together again. If necessary, make a conscious effort to pull in the stomach slightly.
5. Breathe in deeply: "One . . . two . . . three . . . four."
6. Let the air out slowly: "One . . . two . . . three . . . four."
7. Repeat this five more times.
8. Open your eyes.
9. How do you feel?

Because this technique is such a quick and convenient way to relax, it can be integrated into a busy and stressful day as many times as may be needed. Use it when you want to become more relaxed and at ease while undertaking a difficult task. Take a three to five minute "time-out" whenever you need to.

VISUAL IMAGERY: Achieving Mental Relaxation

In reducing stress, it's as necessary and important to relax the mind as it is the body. Visual imagery — sometimes called guided imagery or visualization — is a powerful tool for doing that.

The goals of imagery are to reduce and control mental anxiety. Visual imagery is used to produce positive, relaxing images and thoughts, and to block out intruding and upsetting ones. For example, you may be physically tired and yet be unable to sleep because of upsetting thoughts. By using pleasant visual images, you can control upsetting thoughts and enjoy a deep state of relaxation.

Learning to control your thoughts involves knowing what you need to think about, practicing those thoughts, and then using them when you want to relax. To become proficient at visual imagery, it's helpful to begin with exercises that proceed from simple to more complex images.

Mental imagery is a little like a daydream. You may want to start by trying to visualize a calming, pleasant scene, perhaps one you have seen many times. Try to re-experience the scene in every way you can, including the use of images from senses such as smell (for example, the scent of flowers), touch (the feel of the grass beneath your feet), sound (the singing of birds in the trees), and taste (the salt air at the beach). Soothing music can also be used to achieve a calm state.

Each step is a plateau in the learning of imagery. Be patient with yourself as you begin to learn mental relaxation. Complete concentration, even on pleasant images, requires a great deal of practice. Don't get upset if unwanted thoughts come to your mind — simply redirect them. To prepare, find a quiet place without distractions. Sit or lie down. Get comfortable.

Here are the steps:

1. Close your eyes.
2. Relax your muscles. (You might want to add progressive muscle relaxation or the breathing exercises here.)
3. Take a deep breath. Imagine breathing in the clean air. As you breathe out, feel the relaxation spread over your body. As you take another breath, feel yourself floating down.
4. Tense and relax your muscles.
5. Imagine yourself doing something relaxing. Create that picture in your mind. Imagine it in every detail. Look around and notice the colors in your surroundings, the air on your skin, the warmth of the sun, the sounds, and the odors. Make it as real as possible, and linger as long as you like. Here are some ideas:

   ■ You are lying on the beach, warm under the sun. The sand feels soft and smooth underneath you. You're very calm and relaxed, almost falling asleep. The ocean breeze feels good against your skin. You can taste the salt air on your lips. You can hear the waves rolling in gently. You feel very comfortable, relaxed, peaceful, and calm . . . .

   ■ You are walking slowly through a beautiful green forest. All you hear are birds and the waterfall in the distance. It's very peaceful, and you continue to walk slowly and quietly, enjoying the calm and peacefulness. It's a warm day, but the forest is very comfortable. You have the forest all to yourself with nothing to disturb you. You begin to hum your favorite tune . . . .

   ■ It is a lazy Saturday morning. A cool rain is falling outside, making gentle sounds that can be heard against your window. You are still sleepy. You bask in the thought of not having to get up, and begin to daydream about . . . .

6. When you are ready to end your mental escape, stretch your arms, take a deep breath, and open your eyes.

Creating Your Own Images

Only you know the images that are most relaxing for you. Once you are able to visualize freely, create your own relaxing picture. Here are the basics:

■ Imagine you're in a fantasy spot — some place that is perfect in every way. See all the details, such as people, buildings, animals, sounds, motions that make your fantasy spot ideal. It may be a place you've always wanted to visit, it may be an experience you've always wished for, like being on a yacht or some romantic island — whatever you can imagine that really satisfies you.

■ Imagine a special place where you always feel peaceful, safe and comfortable — and where there is a special friend who understands you and with whom you can talk. This can be a real or an imaginary place — perhaps your grandmother's home with the smell of cinnamon rolls baking in the oven; or a special, safe hiding place that only you know about. Imagine yourself talking to your special friend and telling him or her all your problems. You friend is very wise, and as you talk, imagine your tensions dissolving away.

These guidelines can get you started.

1. Name a place that makes you feel relaxed.
2. Put yourself in a beautiful and serene setting. What are you doing?
3. What's the weather like there?
4. How do you feel when you are there?
5. Why would you like to return?

Visual imagery can be used for tasks other than relaxing. As you see yourself in a conflict or problem situation, try to imagine yourself dealing successfully with the situation. When you choose your thoughts, you have a better chance to be in charge of your emotions and are more likely to be in control of your behavior. If you mentally practice talking over a discipline problem with a rambunctious student, or being assertive with a supervisor or colleague, you'll find that actually playing out the scene is much easier and less stressful than you had anticipated.

THE 30 SECOND "INSTANT RELAXER"

Being short on time can make you feel tense. Here's a 30 second "instant" way to relax:

1. Sit comfortably, both feet on the floor, hands loosely in your lap.
2. Take a deep breath.
3. Let your jaw relax open, and exhale with a deep sigh.
4. Take another deep breath.
5. Let your jaw relax open, and exhale with a deep sigh.
6. Take another deep breath.
7. Let your jaw relax open, and exhale with a deep sigh.

DEEP MUSCLE RELAXATION

Here's a short version of muscle relaxation that is also very effective:

1. Sit comfortably, both feet on the floor, hands loosely in your lap.
2. Take a deep breath and clench your fists as tightly as you can.
3. Hold to the count of five — then exhale and relax your hands. Notice how your hands feel when they're relaxed.
4. Take another deep breath and tighten up your face — tighten your nose and mouth and forehead as much as you can.
5. Hold to the count of five, then exhale and relax your face and jaw — notice the difference.
6. Take another deep breath and tighten your stomach and buttocks — tighten them as much as you can.
7. Hold to the count of five, then exhale and relax.
8. Take another deep breath and tighten your legs. Press them close them together as close as you can.
9. Hold to the count of five — then exhale and relax.
10. Take another deep breath and tighten your feet and ankles.
11. Hold to the count of five — then exhale and relax.
12. Now, take another deep breath and tighten your entire body making it as rigid and stiff as you can.
13. Hold to the count of five — then exhale deeply and relax your body.
14. Let it sink into the chair and notice the difference when your body is completely relaxed.

PROFESSIONAL ASSISTANCE

There are times when another sympathetic individual is not able to give you all the help you need. Although many stress-related symptoms clear up when the stressor is removed or the emotional difficulty subsides, chronic problems may require the attention of a specialist. Severe depression or overwhelming work, family or emotional problems, drug or alcohol abuse are examples of problems that should be dealt with under the guidance of a professional. A counselor will not tell you how to live your life, but he or she can provide guidelines to follow in evaluating your situation. Through tests and questionnaires administered by a skilled professional in the area of stress, you can learn what health concerns loom; through counseling, you can learn how best to reduce those hazards.

How to Find a Counselor or Therapist

You can find a counselor in several ways. Ask friends who have been through counseling to give you the names of those who have helped them. Look in the Yellow Pages under "Psychologists" or "Counselors." Additionally, your Employee Assistance Program, counseling referral service, church, synagogue, all can give you the names of qualified professionals.

Concerns about cost shouldn't keep you from getting help. Health insurance policies usually cover psychological services. Universities and colleges often have psychiatric or psychology departments that run counseling centers at very low cost, as do YMCA's and community agencies. Many therapists work on a sliding scale fee. Counseling comes in all price ranges.

Guidelines for Choosing a Therapist

■ Is he or she a licensed psychotherapist who is respected by the professional community and general public?

■ Does the therapist have a pleasant disposition, a sense of humor, and appear to be functioning well in their own personal life?

■ Do you feel safe, comfortable, and at ease with this person?

■ Is the therapist willing to explain his or her approach to your problem, as well as goals and probable length of treatment?

In addition to assisting you through the current crisis, a good therapist will also help you learn new skills that you can continue to use in the future.

Places to Look for a Counselor or Therapist

■ Company Employee Assistance Program

■ Counseling Referral Service

■ Yellow Pages under Psychologists or Counselors

■ Church or synagogue, YMCA

■ University psychiatric or psychology departments

Tracking your stress and keeping records on the effectiveness of the coping techniques is an excellent way to sharpen your skills in managing stress. Over time you'll not only see the results but feel them as well. But of course, it's up to *you* to do it!

COMMITMENT TO CHANGE

For stress management skills to be of use, you must incorporate them into your work patterns and lifestyle. How helpful they are and how much you benefit will depend on how much effort you invest in the process.

No one can compel you to responsibly take care of yourself. Only you can make that decision. "Nothing great is lightly won." Ever hear that cliche? Like many others, it's a cliche because it contains enough truth to make it worth saying over and over. Nothing great is lightly won. What could be greater than living a stress-free, relaxed, productive life? Isn't one of your goals as a professional to be as competent and efficient as possible, and one of your goals as a human being to be content and relaxed with yourself? These are excellent, worthwhile goals . . . which are not lightly won.

Being responsible for yourself involves effort, dedication, and *commitment*. You have to face yourself and say, "I'm in control. No one knows what's better for me than I do. No one else should be put in charge of managing my life. It's up to me."

Like the Nike expression says, "Just Do It!" Luckily, *you can*!

We've been discussing some of the many ways to alleviate stress. Of course there are many others. For example, one of the central concepts in coping with stress is to recognize the role expectations play in giving a person either a feeling of gratification or frustration. Right along with this comes the need to adopt a much greater degree of personal gratitude and thankfulness for what one has, for what one has accomplished, and for the freedom each of us has to decide our future. Whether we call our activity exhausting work or relaxing play depends largely upon our own attitude towards it. We need to be on friendly terms with our life.

We can also dissipate stress by an act of will, by placing ourselves mentally at a distance so we can look at the stressful situation dispassionately, then deliberately seeing the humorous side and laughing. It's one of the greatest secrets: To take oneself and one's importance in the total scheme of things less seriously than a person ordinarily does. Yet an important judgment enters in: The need to recognize that sometimes a single individual makes the critical difference in the outcome of an event. Intuition can tell you when to take yourself seriously, and when not to.

There are many other possibilities that could make a difference in our stress levels. We could for example:

■ Improve in-service workshops and teacher preparation education.

■ Form cadres of teacher researchers who are assigned to work on classroom problems.

■ Revitalize our careers periodically — to change those activities we dislike and improve those activities we enjoy.

■ Consider a sabbatical — write to curriculum groups, to exchange programs, to the state department of education, to federal grant-giving agencies or other organizations to determine our options.

■ Visit other schools and classrooms during the school year.

■ Teach at a university in a summer program.

■ Hire older students to do routine clerical work.

■ Elect a preretirement plan.

■ Make your classroom attractive. Try growing something green (not mold!). Put an area rug on the floor. Hang some of your favorite pictures. Get a bookcase that doesn't look like it was issued by the U.S. army. Bring in some sound (other than the students) like a radio or stereo. You spend a great deal of time in your classroom, so make it pleasant.

■ Have lunch with someone other than your usual group.

■ Stop being a slave to routine.

■ Avoid mean and stupid people. I know I'm not supposed to say that, but you must admit, there are always a couple of staff members you just can't please and who just won't participate. After you've tried to bolster their self-esteem and you find they won't return the gesture, stay clear of them. They'll dislike you no more or less.

A CONTRACT WITH MYSELF & MY FUTURE

I, _____, wishing to improve my overall health and knowing that there is a relationship between my physical and mental well-being and the level of my everyday stress, hereby make a commitment to myself to carry out the following stress-management program over the course of the next month. I will:

- Keep a *Daily Exercise and Diet Log*, which will provide me with a graphic portrayal of the interaction between my daily activities and my stress symptoms.

- Make changes in my lifestyle as necessary: Reduce or eliminate smoking from my life alto-gether, moderate my intake of alcoholic beverages if needed, reexamine the purpose of drugs I may be taking.

- Undertake a program of regular exercise.

- Review my own belief system and those of people close to me to determine whether we are raising each other's stress levels by imposing our judgmental thoughts or rigid ideas on one another.

(continue here with your own list)

- _____

- _____

- _____

- _____

- _____

- _____

- _____

- _____

In short, I hereby assert that I will to the best of my ability take charge of my own life and health by making changes where I see areas of potential harm to myself or others.

To make this contract more binding, I will make out a check for $25 to an organization I cannot endorse. I will give this check to a friend whom I trust and admire with the instructions to ask me in one month whether I have met the terms of this contract. If I have not, this person will be instructed to give my check to the organization whose beliefs I cannot endorse. If I have met the terms of this contract, I may use the $25 in any enjoyable way I see fit. I will repeat this process monthly.

_____ Date _____

(Signature)

Resources and Suggested Readings

Ackoff, R. *The Art of Problem Solving.* New York: John Wiley and Sons, 1978.

Anderson, E., G. Tedman, and C. Rogers. *Self-Esteem for Tots to Teens.* New York: Meadowbrook/Simon and Schuster, 1984.

Anglund, J. W. *A Friend Is Someone Who Likes You.* New York: Hartcourt and Brace, 1985.

Axline, V. M. *Dibs: In Search of Self.* New York: Ballantine Books, 1967.

Barksdale, L. S. *Essays on Self-Esteem.* Idyllwild, CA: The Barksdale Foundation, 1977.

Baron, J. B., and R. J. Sternberg, Robert J., Ed. *Teaching Thinking Skills: Theory and Practice.* New York: W. H. Freeman and Co., 1987.

Baron, J. D. *Kids and Drugs.* New York: Putnam, 1983.

Beane, J., and R. Lipka. *Self Concept, Self-Esteem and the Curriculum.* New York: Teachers College Press, 1984.

Bedley, G. *The ABCD's of Discipline.* Irvine, CA: People-Wise Publications, 1979.

Bennett, W. *Schools Without Drugs.* U.S. Department of Education: White House, Washington, D.C., 1989.

Bergstrom, C. *Losing Your Best Friend: Losing Friendship.* New York: Human Science Press, 1984.

Berne, E. *What Do You Say After You Say Hello?* New York: Grove Press, 1971.

Berne, P., and L. Savary. *Building Self-Esteem in Children.* New York: Continuum, 1989.

Bessell, H., and T. Kelly, Jr. *The Parent Book.* Rolling Hills Estates, CA: Jalmar Press, 1977.

Betancourt, J. *Am I Normal?* New York: Avon, 1983.

Bingham, E. E., and S. J. Stryker. *CHOICES: A Teen Woman's Journal for Self-Awareness and Personal Planning.* El Toro, CA: Mission Publications, 1985.

Bingham, E. E., and S. J. Stryker. *CHOICES: A Teen Man's Journal for Self-Awareness and Personal Planning.* El Toro, CA: Mission Publications, 1985.

Bloom, Benjamin. S. "Affective Outcomes of School Learning." *Phi Delta Kappa,* 1977: pp. 193—199.

Blume, J. *Are You There, God? It's Me, Margaret.* New York: Dell, 1970.

Blume, J. *Then Again, Maybe I Won't.* New York: Dell, 1971.

Booraem, C., J. Flowers, and B. Schwartz. *Help Your Children Be Self-Confident.* Englewood Cliffs, NJ: Prentice-Hall, Inc., 1978.

Bonny, H., and L. Savary. *Music and Your Mind.* New York: Harper & Row, 1973.

Borba, M. *Esteem Builders.* Rolling Hills Estates, CA: Jalmar Press, 1989.

Bradley, B. *Where Do I Belong? A Kid's Guide to Stepfamilies.* Reading, MA: Addison-Wesley, 1982.

Branden, N. *Psychology of Self-Esteem.* Los Angeles: Bantam Books, Nash Publishing Co., 1969.

Branden, N. *"What is Self-Esteem?"* First International Conference on Self-Esteem: August 1990, Asker, Norway. Paper presented.

Briggs, D. C. *Your Child's Self-Esteem.* New York: Dolphin Books, Doubleday & Company, 1975.

Briggs, D. C. *Celebrate Yourself.* Garden City, NY: Doubleday, 1977.

Brookover, W. B. *Self-Concept of Ability and School Achievement.* East Lansing, MI: Office of Research and Public Info., Michigan State University, 1965.

Buntman, P. H. *How to Live With Your Teenager.* New York: Ballantine Books, 1979.

Buscaglia, L. *Living, Loving & Learning.* Thorofare, NJ: Charles B. Slack, 1982.

Buscaglia, L. *Love.* Thorofare, NJ: Charles B. Slack, 1972.

Canfield, J., and H. C. Wells. *100 Ways to Enhance Self-Concept in the Classroom.* Englewood Cliffs, NJ: Prentice-Hall, 1976.

Cathcart, R. S. *Small Group Communication.* Dubuque, IA: Wm. C. Brown Company, 1979.

Cetron, M. *Schools of the Future.* New York: McGraw Hill, 1985.

"Children Having Children: Teen Pregnancy in America." *TIME.* December 9, 1985, pp. 78—90.

Chuska, K. R. *Teaching the Process of Thinking, K-12.* Bloomington, Indiana: Phi Delta Kappa Educational Foundation, 1986.

Clems, H., and R. Bean. *Self-Esteem The Key to Your Child's Well-Being.* New York: Putnam, 1981.

Coopersmith, S. *The Antecedents of Self-Esteem.* San Francisco, CA: W. H. Freeman, 1967.

Covington, M. "Self-Esteem and Failure in School." *The Social Importance of Self-Esteem.* University of California Press, Berkeley, CA, 1989.

Cretcher, D. *Steering Clear.* Minneapolis, MN: Winston, 1982.

Crockenberg, S., and B. Soby. "Self-Esteem and Teenage Pregnancy," *The Social Importance of Self-Esteem.* University of California Press, Berkeley, CA, 1989.

Crow, L., and A. Crow. *How to Study.* New York: Collier Books, 1980.

Curran, D. *Traits of a Healthy Family.* Minneapolis, MN: Winston, 1983.

Danziger, P. *The Cat Ate My Gymsuit.* New York: Dell, 1973.

Davis, L., and J. Davis. *How to Live Almost Happily With Your Teenagers.* Minneapolis, MN: Winston, 1982.

Dillon, J. T. *Teaching and The Art of Questioning.* Bloomington, IN: Phi Delta Kappa Educational Foundation, 1983.

Dishon, D., and P. W. O'Leary. *A Guidebook for Cooperative Learning: A Technique for Creating More Effective Schools.* Holmes Beach, FL: Learning Publications, Inc., 1984.

"Do You Know What Your Children Are Listening To?" *U.S. News & World Report.* October 28, 1985.

Dobson, J. *Preparing for Adolescence.* Santa Ana, CA: Vision House, 1978.

Dodson, F. *How to Discipline With Love.* New York: Rawson Associates, 1977.

Dreikurs, R. *Children: The Challenge.* New York: Hawthorn, 1964.

Drew, N. *Learning the Skills of Peacemaking.* Rolling Hills Estates, CA: Jalmar Press, 1987.

Dyer, W. *What Do You Really Want for Your Children?* New York: William Morrow and Company, Inc., 1985.

Earle, J. *Female Dropouts: A New Perspective.* Alexandria, VA: National Association of State Boards of Education, 1987.

Elkind, D. *All Grown Up and No Place to Go*. Reading, MA: Addison-Wesley, 1984.

"Family Fitness: A Complete Exercise Program for Ages Six to Sixty-Plus." *Reader's Digest*. (Special Report) 1987, pp. 2-12.

Fensterheim, H. *Don't Say Yes When You Want to Say No*. New York: Dell Publishing Co., 1975.

Fox, L., and F. Lavin-Weaver. *Unlocking Doors to Self-Esteem*. Rolling Hills Estates, CA: Jalmar Press, 1983.

Freed, A. *TA for Tots*. Revised. Rolling Hills Estates, CA: Jalmar Press, 1991.

Freed, A. *TA for Teens*. Rolling Hills Estates, CA: Jalmar Press, 1976.

Freed, A., and M. Freed. *TA for Kids*. Rolling Hills Estates, CA: Jalmar Press, 1977.

Fromm, Eric. *The Art of Loving*. New York: Bantam, 1963.

Fugitt, E. D. *He Hit Me Back First!* Rolling Hills Estates, CA: Jalmar Press, 1983.

Gall, M. "Synthesis of Research on Teachers' Questioning," *Educational Leadership*. November 1984, pp. 40-47.

Gardner, J. E. *Turbulent Teens*. Rolling Hills Estates, CA: Jalmar Press, 1983.

Gardner, R. *The Boys and Girls Book About Stepfamilies*. New York: Bantam Books, 1982.

Gelb, M. *Present Yourself*. Rolling Hills Estates, CA: Jalmar Press, 1988.

Getzoff, A., and C. McClenahan. *Stepkids: A Survival Guide for Teenagers in Stepfamilies*. New York: Walker and Company, 1984.

Gibbs, J. *Tribes: A Process for Social Development and Cooperative Learning*. Center Source Publications: Santa Rosa, CA, 1987.

Ginott, H. *Teacher and Child*. New York: Avon, 1972.

Gimbel, C. *Why Does Santa Claus Celebrate Christmas?* Rolling Hills Estates, CA: Jalmar Press, 1990.

Glasser, W. *Schools Without Failure*. New York: Harper & Row, 1969.

Gordon, T. *Parent Effectiveness Training*. New York: Peter H. Wyden, 1974.

Gossop, M. "Drug Dependence and Self-Esteem," *International Journal of Addictions*, Vol. II, 1976.

Greenberg, P. *I Know I'm Myself Because . . .* New York: Human Science Press, 1988.

Gribben, T. *Pajamas Don't Matter*. Rolling Hills Estates, CA: Jalmar Press, 1979

Harris, T. A. *I'm OK—You're OK*. New York: Avon, 1967.

"Has Rock Gone Too Far?" *People Magazine*. September 16, 1985, pp. 47-53.

Haynes-Klassen. *Learning to Live, Learning to Love*. Rolling Hills Estates, CA: Jalmar Press, 1985.

Hill, W. F. *Learning Through Discussion*. Beverly Hills, CA: Sage Publications, 1977.

Holt, J. *How Children Learn*. New York: Delta Books, 1967.

Hyde, M. O. *Parents Divided, Parents Multiplied*. Louisville, KY: Westminster/John Knox Press, 1989.

James, M., and D. Jongeward. *Born to Win*. Menlo Park, CA: Addison-Wesley, 1971.

Jampolsky, G. G. *Teach Only Love*. New York: Bantam, 1983.

Johnson, D. W., and R. T. Johnson *Learning Together and Alone: Cooperative, Competitive and Individualistic Learning*, 4th ed. Englewood Cliffs, NJ: Prentice-Hall, Inc., 1987.

Johnson, D. W., R. T. Johnson, E. J. Holubec, and P. Roy. *Circles of Learning*. ASCD Publications, 1984.

Kagan, S. *Cooperative Learning Resources for Teachers*. Riverside, CA: School of Education, University of California, 1985.

Kalb, J., and Viscott, D. *What Every Kid Should Know*. Boston: Houghton Mifflin, 1974.

Kaplan, H. B. *Self-Attitudes and Deviant Behavior*. Goodyear, Pacific Palisades, CA, 1975.

Kaufman, R. *Identifying and Solving Problems: A System Approach*. San Diego, CA: University Associates, Inc., 1989.

Kehayan, V. Alex. *Partners For Change*. Rolling Hills Estates, CA: Jalmar Press, 1992.

Kehayan, V. Alex. *SAGE: Self-Awareness Growth Experiences*. Rolling Hills Estates, CA: Jalmar Press, 1989.

Keirsey, D., and M. Bates. *Please Understand Me*. Del Mar, CA: Prometheus Nemesis, 1978.

Kelley, T. M. "Changes in Self-Esteem Among Pre-Delinquent Youths in Voluntary Counseling Relationships." *Juvenile and Family Court Journal*. Vol. 29, May, 1978.

"Kids and Cocaine: An Epidemic Strikes Middle America." *Newsweek*. March 17, 1986, pp. 58-63.

Knight, M. E., T. L. Graham, R. A. Juliano, S. R. Miksza, and P. G. Tonnies. *Teaching Children to Love Themselves*. Englewood Cliffs, NJ: Prentice-Hall, 1982.

Kohen-Raz, R. *The Child from 9—13*. Chicago Illinois: Aldine Adterton, Inc., 1971.

Kreidler, W. *Creative Conflict Resolution: More Than 200 Activities for Keeping Peace in the Classroom*. Glenview, IL: Scott, Foresman and Co., 1984.

Lalli, J. *Feelings Alphabet*. Rolling Hills Estates, CA: Jalmar Press, 1988.

Lansky, D, and S. Dorfman. *How To Survive High School with Minimal Brain Damage*. Minneapolis, MN: Meadowbrook, 1989.

LeShan, E. *What's Going to Happen to Me? When Parents Separate or Divorce*. Four Winds Press, 1978.

Lewis, D., and J. Greene. *Thinking Better*. New York: Rawson, Wade Publishers, Inc., 1982.

Lorayne, H., and J. Lucas. *The Memory Book*. New York: Stein and Day, 1974.

Kuczen, B. *Childhood Stress*. New York: Delacarte, 1982.

Male, M., D. Johnson, R. Johnson, and M. Anderson. *Cooperative Learning and Computers: An Activity Guide for Teachers*. CA: Educational-Apple-Cations, 1987.

Martinelli, K. J. "Thinking Straight About Thinking," *The School Administrator*, No. 44, January 1987, pp. 21-23.

Maslow, A. *Toward a Psychology of Being*. New York: D. Van Nostrand, 1962.

McCabe, M. E., and J. Rhoades. *How to Say What You Mean*. CA: ITA Publications, 1985.

McCullough, C., and R. Mann. *Managing Your Anxiety*. Los Angeles, CA: Tarcher/St. Martins Press, 1985.

McDaniel, S., and P. Bielen. *Project Self-Esteem*. Rolling Hills Estates, CA: Jalmar Press, 1990.

McKay, M., and P. Fanning. *Self-Esteem*. Oakland, CA: New Harbinger Publications, 1987.

Miller, G. P. *Teaching Your Child To Make Decisions*. New York: Harper & Row, 1984.

Montessori, M. *The Discovery of the Child*. Notre Dame, IN: Fides, 1967.

Moore, Ph.D., G. B., and Serby, T. *Becoming Whole Through Games* Rolling Hills Estates, CA: Jalmar Press, 1988.

Naisbitt, J. *Megatrends*. New York: Warner Books, 1982.

Newman, M., and B. Berkowitz. *How to Be Your Own Best Friend*. New York: Random House, 1973.

Neufeld, J. *Lisa, Bright and Dark*. New York: S. G. Phillips, 1969.

Olson, C. B. "Fostering Critical Thinking Skills Through Writing," *Educational Leadership*, November 1984, pp. 28—39.

Palmer, P. *Liking Myself*. San Luis Obispo, CA: Impact, 1977.

Palmer, Pat. *The Mouse, The Monster, and Me*. San Luis Obispo, CA: Impact, 1977.

Peal, N. V. *You Can If You Think You Can*. Pawling, NY: Foundation for Christian Living, 1974.

Pelletier, K. *Mind as Healer, Mind as Slayer*. New York: Delacorte, 1977.

Postman, N. *The Disappearance of Childhood*. New York: Delacorte Press, 1982.

Raths, L. E., et al. *Teaching for Thinking: Theories, Strategies, and Activities for the Classroom*. New York: Teachers College Press, 1986.

Richards, A. K., and I. Willis. *Boy Friends, Girl Friends, Just Friends*. Atheneum, NY: McClelland & Stewart, Ltd., 1979.

Samples, B. *Metaphoric Mind*. Rolling Hills Estates, CA: Jalmar Press, 1991.

Samples, B. *Openmind/Wholemind*. Rolling Hills Estates, CA: Jalmar Press, 1987.

Samson, R. W. *Thinking Skills: A Guide to Logic and Comprehension*. Stamford, CT: Innovative Sciences, Inc., 1981.

Satir, V. *Peoplemaking*. Palo Alto, CA: Science & Behavior Books, Inc., 1972.

Schmuck, R., and P. Schmuck. *A Humanistic Psychology of Education: Making the School Everybody's House*. Palo Alto, CA: Mayfield Publishing Co., 1974.

Schneiderwind, N., and E. Davidson. *Open Minds to Equity: A Soucebook of Learning Activities to Promote Race, Sex, Class and Age Equity*. NJ: Prentice-Hall, 1983.

Schuller, R. *Self-Esteem: The New Reformation*. Waco, TX: Word Books, Inc., 1982.

Schriner, C. *Feel Better Now*. Rolling Hills Estates, CA: Jalmar Press, 1990.

Sexton, T. G., and D. R. Poling. "Can Intelligence Be Taught?" Bloomingdale, IN: Phi Delta Kappa Educational Foundation, 1973.

Sheehy, G. *Pathfinders,* New York: Morrow, 1981.

Sheinkin, D. *Food, Mind and Mood*. New York: Warner Books, 1980.

Shles, L. *Aliens in My Nest*. Rolling Hills Estates, CA: Jalmar Press, 1988.

Shles, L. *Moths & Mothers/Feathers & Fathers*. Rolling Hills Estates, CA: Jalmar Press, 1989.

Shles, L. *Do I Have to Go to School Today?* Rolling Hills Estates, CA: Jalmar Press, 1989.

Shles, L. *Hugs & Shrugs*. Rolling Hills Estates, CA: Jalmar Press, 1987.

Shles, L. *Hoots & Toots & Hairy Brutes?* Rolling Hills Estates, CA: Jalmar Press, 1989.

Silberstein, W. *Helping Your Child Grow Slim*. New York: Simon & Schuster, 1982.

Simpson, B. K. *Becoming Aware of Values*. La Mesa, CA: Pennant Press, 1973.

Skoguland, E. R. *To Anger With Love*. New York: Harper & Row, 1977.

Smith, M. J. *When I Say No I Feel Guilty*. New York: Bantam, 1975.

Sparks, A. H. *Two Minute Lover*. Rolling Hills Estates, CA: Jalmar Press, 1989.

Stainback, W., and S. Stainback. *How to Help Your Child Succeed in School*. Minneapolis, MN: Meadowbrook, 1988.

Steffenhagen, R. A., and J. D. Burns. *The Social Dynamics of Self-Esteem*. New York, NY: Praeger, 1987.

Steiner, C. *The Original Warm Fuzzy Tale*. Rolling Hills Estates, CA: Jalmar Press, 1977.

"Teenage Fathers." *Psychology Today*. December, 1985. pp. 66—70.

Ungerleider, D. *Reading, Writing and Rage*. Rolling Hills Estates, CA: Jalmar Press, 1985.

Vennard, J. *Synergy*. Novato, CA: Academic Therapy Publications, 1978.

Viscott, D. *The Language of Feelings*. New York: Pocket Books, 1976.

Vitale, B. M. *Unicorns Are Real*. Rolling Hills Estates, CA: Jalmar Press, 1982.

Vitale, B. M. *Free Flight*. Rolling Hills Estates, CA: Jalmar Press, 1986.

Waas, Ph.D., L. L. *Imagine That!* Rolling Hills Estates, CA: Jalmar Press, 1991.

Wahlross, S. *Family Communication*. New York: Macmillan Publishing Co., Inc., 1974.

Warren, N. C. *Make Anger Your Ally*. Garden City, NY: Doubleday, 1983.

Wassmer, A. C. *Making Contact*. New York: Dial Press, 1978.

Whitely, J. *Moral Character Development of College Students*. University of Irvine, Irvine, CA, 1980.

Wilson, J. "Motivation, Modeling, and Altruism," *Journal of Personality and Social Psychology*, Vol. 34, December 1976.

Winn, M. *Children Without Childhood*. New York: Pantheon Books, 1981.

Winter, A., and R. Winter. *Build Your Brain Power*. New York: St. Martin's, 1986.

Wright, E. *Good Morning Class — I Love You!* Rolling Hills Estates, CA: Jalmar Press, 1989.

Wyckoff, J, and B. Unell. *Discipline Without Shouting or Spanking*. Minneapolis, MN: Meadowbrook, 1988.

Young, E. *I Am a Blade of Grass*. Rolling Hills Estates, CA: Jalmar Press, 1989.

Youngs, Bettie B. *Stress in Children: How to Recognize, Avoid and Overcome It*. New York: Avon, 1985.

Youngs, Bettie B. *Helping Your Teenager Deal With Stress. A Guide to the Adolescent Years*. Los Angeles, CA: Tarcher/St. Martins, 1986

Youngs, Bettie B. *Is Your Net-Working? A Complete Guide to Building Contacts and Career Visibility*. New York: John Wiley & Sons, 1989.

Youngs, Bettie B. *Friendship Is Forever, Isn't It?* Rolling Hills Estates, CA: Jalmar Press, 1990.

Youngs, Bettie B. *The 6 Vital Ingredients of Self-Esteem and How to Develop Them in Your Child.* New York: Macmillan, 1992.

Youngs, Bettie B. *The 6 Vital Ingredients of Self-Esteem and How to Develop Them in Your Students.* Rolling Hills Estates, CA: Jalmar Press, 1992.

Youngs, Bettie B. *Enhancing The Educator's Self-Esteem. It's Your Criteria #1.* Rolling Hills Estates, CA: Jalmar Press: 1992.

Youngs, Bettie B. *Goal Setting Skills for Young People.* Rolling Hills Estates, CA: Jalmar Press, second edition, 1992 .

Youngs, Bettie B. *You and Self-Esteem: It's The Key to Happiness & Success.* Rolling Hills Estates, CA: Jalmar Press, 1992.

Youngs, Bettie B. *A Stress Management Guide for Young People.* Rolling Hills Estates, CA: Jalmar Press, second edition, 1993.

Youngs, Bettie B. *Problem Solving Skills for Children.* Rolling Hills Estates, CA: Jalmar Press, second edition, 1993.

Youngs, Bettie B. *Stress Management for Administrators.* Rolling Hills Estates, CA: Jalmar Press, 1993.

Youngs, Bettie B. *The Teenager: A Guide to the Adolescent Years.* Deerfield Beach, FL: Health Communications, 1993.

Help Organizations

Many organizations, some with toll-free 800 phone numbers, provide helpful information, among them:

Alcoholics Anonymous
World Services, Inc.
468 Park Ave. South
New York, NY 10016
(212) 686-1100

Al-Ateen, Al-Anon Family Group Headquarters
P.O. Box 182
New York, NY 10159-0182

Alcoholics Anonymous is an international fellowship of men and women who share the common problem of alcoholism. Family members of alcoholics can receive help through groups associated with Alcoholics Anonymous, mainly Al-Anon and Al-Ateen. Al-Ateen chapters are listed in some phone books or you can contact a local Al-Anon group for more information.

Big Brothers/Big Sisters of America
230 North Thirteenth St.
Philadelphia, PA 19107
(215) 567-7000

Big Brothers/Big Sisters of America is a national youth-serving organization based on the concept of a one-to-one relationship between an adult volunteer and an at-risk child, usually from a one-parent family. With more than 495 agencies located nationwide, the organization is dedicated to providing children and youth with adult role models and mentors who help enrich the children's lives, as well as their own, through weekly interaction. Volunteers go through a screening process before being accepted into the program, and professional caseworkers provide assistance, support, and on-going supervision for all matches. Check the white pages of your phone book for the agency nearest you.

Boys' National Hotline
(800) 448-3000 (toll-free)
This hot line provides emergency crisis counseling.

Family Service America (FSA)
11700 West Lake Park Drive
Park Place
Milwaukee, WI 53224
(414) 359-1040

FSA is a membership organization of agencies that deals with family problems serving more than 1000 communities throughout the United States and Canada. Member agencies serve families and individuals through counseling, advocacy, and family life education. Consult the phone book for the agency nearest you.

National Center for Missing and Exploited Children
2101 Wilson Blvd., Ste. 550
Arlington, VA 22021
(703) 235-3900

The center assists families, citizens' groups, law enforcement agencies, and governmental institutions. The center also has a toll-free number for reporting information that could lead to the location and recovery of a missing child. The number is (800) 843-5678.

National Child Abuse Hotline
P.O. Box 630
Hollywood, CA 90028
(800) 422-4453 (toll-free)

The National Child Abuse Hotline handles crises calls and information and offers referrals to every county in the United States. The hot line is manned by professionals holding a master's degree or Ph.D. in psychology. The hot line also provides literature about child abuse prevention. This program is sponsored by Childhelp USA, which is located in Woodland, CA.

National Clearinghouse for Alcohol and Drug Information (NCADI)
P.O. Box 2345
Rockville, MD 20852
(301) 468-2600
(800) 729-6686 (toll-free)

NCADI is the information component of the Office for Substance Abuse Prevention (OSAP) of the U.S. Dept. of Health and Human Services. The clearinghouse maintains an inventory of hundreds of publications developed by federal agencies and private sector organizations. Most publications are free or are available in bulk quantities for a small fee. NCADI also offers fact verification, video loans, and dissemination of grant announcements and application kits. NCADI provides access to the Prevention Materials Database, an on-line computer database designed to help select specific items from the NCADI's collection of prevention materials. NCADI publishes "Prevention Pipeline," a bimonthly publication that contains the latest information about research, resources, and activities within the prevention field.

National Council for Self-Esteem
P.O. Box 277877
Sacramento, CA 95827-7877
(916) 455-NCSE
(916) 454-2000

The NCSE is dedicated to promoting and developing quality self-esteem information. The NCSE's mission is to spread the ethics of self-esteem throughout the United States. The organization seeks to ensure that self-esteem information is readily available to those who seek it. Operating as Self-Esteem Central, the NSCE collects information on the best self-esteem curriculums, school programs, drug prevention programs, drop-out prevention programs, study courses, videos, and audio tape programs. Self-Esteem Central houses the National Self-Esteem Library, reported to be be the largest collection of self-esteem resources in the world. The library offers research assistance and audio tape programs. The "Self-Esteem Today" newsletter offers the latest in new ideas to develop self-esteem, including current research, model programs, and upcoming conference information. More than 50 local Self-Esteem Councils exist in twenty states. For more information, or to start a council in your city, write the NSCE.

National Institute on Drug Abuse
P.O. Box 100
Summit, NJ 07901
(800) COCAINE (toll-free)

The National Institute on Drug Abuse hot line is a confidential drug abuse treatment referral service. The hot line provides information on local referrals and help for drug abusers and other concerned individuals.

National Runaway Switch Board
(800) 621-4000 (toll-free)

National Youth Work Alliance
1346 Connecticut Ave, N.W.
Washington, D.C. 20036
Offers local referrals for runaway or teen crisis shelters.

Parents Anonymous (P.A.)
7120 Franklin
Los Angeles, CA 90046
(800) 421-0353 (toll-free, outside CA)
(800) 352-0386 (toll-free, CA)

P.A. is a self-help program for parents under stress and for abused children. There are no fees and no one is required to reveal his or her name. Group members support and encourage each other in searching out positive alternatives to the abusive behavior in their lives. To locate a P.A. in you area, call the toll-free hotline numbers listed above.

Crisis counseling and information available 24 hours a day, seven days a week.

Stepfamily Association of America, Inc.
215 Centennial Mall South, Suite 212
Lincoln, NE 68508
(402) 477-STEP

Stepfamily Association of America provides education, information, support, and advocacy for stepfamilies. Publications include a quarterly newsletter, *Stepfamilies*, and the book, *Stepfamilies Stepping Ahead*. Local chapters offer classes, workshops, and support groups for stepfamilies. Members of SAA may attend these meetings at no charge.

Suicide Prevention

Almost every state and major city has one or more suicide hotlines and/or suicide prevention centers. For centers in your area, check with your phone operator, or the State, City, or County Health & Human Services headings in your phone book.

United Way, Inc.

Check the phone book to contact the United Way organization in your area to find the Family Services Agency nearest you. These organizations offer a variety of family counseling services.

Notes to Remember

Notes to Remember

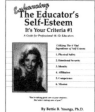

DISCOVER books on self-esteem for kids.

ENJOY great reading with Warm Fuzzies and Squib, the adventurous owl.

Larry Shles, M.A.

Moths & Mothers/Feathers & Fathers: The Story of Squib, The Owl, Begins (Ages 5-105)

Heartwarming story of a tiny owl who cannot fly or hoot as he learns to put words with his feelings. He faces frustration, grief, fear, guilt and loneliness in his life, just as we do. Struggling with these *feelings*, he searches, at least, for *understanding*. *Delightfully illustrated*. Ageless.

0-915190-57-5, 72 pages, **JP-9057-5 $7.95**
8½ x 11, paperback, illustrations

Hoots & Toots & Hairy Brutes: The Continuing Adventures of Squib, The Owl (Ages 5-105)

Squib, who can only toot, sets out to learn how to give a mighty hoot. Even the *owl-odontist* can't help and he fails completely. Every reader who has struggled with *life's limitations* will recognize his own *struggles* and *triumphs* in the microcosm of Squib's forest world. A parable for all ages.

0-915190-56-7, 72 pages, **JP-9056-7 $7.95**
8½ x 11, paperback, illustrations

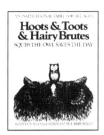

Larry Shles, M.A.

NOT JUST AUTHORS BUT RESEARCHERS AND PRACTITIONERS.

Larry Shles, M.A.

Hugs & Shrugs: The Continuing Saga of Squib, The Owl (Ages 5-105)

Squib feels *lonely, depressed* and *incomplete*. His reflection in the pond shows that he has lost a piece of himself. He thinks his missing piece fell out and he searches in vain outside of himself to find it. Only when he discovers that it fell in and not out does he *find inner-peace* and *become whole*. Delightfully illustrated. Ageless.

0-915190-47-8, 72 pages, **JP-9047-8 $7.95**
8½ x 11, paperback, illustrations

Aliens in my Nest: Squib Meets the Teen Creature (Ages 5-105)

What does it feel like to face a snarly, surly, defiant and non-communicative older brother turned *adolescent*? Friends, dress code, temperament, entertainment, room decor, eating habits, authority, music, isolation, *internal and external conflict* and many other *areas of change* are *dealt with*. Explores how to handle every situation.

0-915190-49-4, 80 pages, **JP-9049-4 $7.95**
8½ x 11, paperback, illustrations

Larry Shles, M.A.

NOT JUST WRITTEN BUT PROVEN EFFECTIVE.

Do I Have to Go to School Today? Squib Measures Up! (Ages 5-105)

Squib *dreads* going to *school*. He day-dreams about all the reasons he has not to go: the school bus will swallow him, the older kids will be mean to him, numbers and letters confuse him, he is too small for sports, etc. But, in the end, he *goes because* his *teacher accepts him "just as he is."* Very esteeming. Great metaphor for all ages.

0-915190-62-1, 64 pages, **JP-9062-1 $7.95**
8½ x 11, paperback, illustrations

Scooter's Tail of Terror A Fable of Addiction and Hope (Ages 5-105)

Well-known author and illustrator, Larry Shles, introduces a new forest character — a squirrel named Scooter. He faces the challenge of addiction, but is offered a way to overcome it. As with the Squib books, the story is *simple*, yet the message is *dramatic*. The story touches the child within each reader and *presents the realities of addiction*.

0-915190-89-3, 80 pages, **JP-9089-3 $9.95**
8½ x 11, paperback, illustrations

NEW

Larry Shles, M.A.

100% TESTED — 100% PRACTICAL — 100% GUARANTEED.

REVISED

Alvyn Freed, Ph.D.

TA for Tots (and other prinzes) Revised (Gr. PreK-3)

Over 500,000 sold. New upright format. Book has helped thousands of young *children* and their *parents* to better *understand* and *relate to each other*. Helps youngsters realize their *intrinsic worth* as human beings; builds and strengthens their *self-esteem. Simple* to understand.
Coloring Book $1.95 / I'm OK Poster $3

0-915190-73-7, 144 pages, **JP-9073-7 $14.95**
8½ x 11, paperback, delightful illustrations

TA for Kids (and grown-ups too) (Gr. 4-9)

Over 250,000 sold. An ideal book to help youngsters *develop self-esteem*, esteem of others, *personal and social responsibility*, critical thinking and independent judgment. Book recognizes that each person is a unique human being with the capacity to learn, grow and develop. Hurray for TA! Great for parents and other care givers.

0-915190-09-5, 112 pages, **JP-9009-5 $9.95**
8½ x 11, paperback, illustrations

Alvyn Freed, Ph.D. & Margaret Freed

ORDER NOW FOR 10% DISCOUNT ON 3 OR MORE TITLES.

TA for Teens (and other important people) (Gr. 8-12)

Over 100,000 sold. The book that tells teenagers they're OK! Provides help in growing into adulthood in a mixed-up world. Contrasts freedom and irresponsibility with knowing that *youth need the skill, determination* and *inner strength* to reach *fulfillment* and *self-esteem*. No talking down to kids, here.

0-915190-03-6, 258 pages, **JP-9003-6 $21.95**
8½ x 11, paperback, illustrations

The Original Warm Fuzzy Tale (Gr. Pre K-Adult)

Over 100,000 sold. The concept of Warm Fuzzies and Cold Pricklies originated in this delightful story. A *fairy tale* in every sense, *with* adventure, fantasy, heroes, villians and a *moral*. Children (and adults, too) will enjoy this beautifully illustrated book. **Songs of Warm Fuzzy Cass. $12.95. Warm Fuzzies, JP-9042 $0.99 each.**

0-915190-08-7, 48 pages, **JP-9008-7 $8.95**
6 x 9, paperback, full color illustrations

Claude Steiner, Ph.D

ORDER FROM: B.L. Winch & Associates/Jalmar Press, Skypark Business Center, 2675 Skypark Drive, Suite 204 , Torrance, CA 90505
CALL TOLL FREE — (800) 662-9662 • (310) 784-0016 • FAX (310) 784-1379 • Add 10% shipping; $3 minimum
2/93

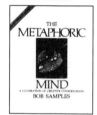